NATURE'S ADVOCATE

A DECADE IN REVIEW

THE CONSERVANCY OF SOUTHWEST FLORIDA IN ITS 60TH YEAR

BY

NICHOLAS G. PENNIMAN IV

Author of Nature's Steward: A History of the Conservancy of Southwest Florida

No part of this publication may be reproduced in whole or in part, or stored in a retrieval system, or transmitted in any form or by any means, electronic, mechanical, photocopying, recording, or otherwise, without written permission of the author, except for the inclusion of brief quotations in a review. For information regarding permission, please write to: info@barringerpublishing.com

Editor's note—Errors and variant spelling in quoted material herein is reproduced as written.

Copyright © 2023
NICHOLAS G. PENNIMAN IV
All rights reserved.

Barringer Publishing, Naples, Florida
www.barringerpublishing.com
Design and layout by Linda S. Duider

ISBN 978-1-954396-61-6

Library of Congress Cataloging-in-Publication Data
Nature's Advocate: *A Decade in Review*

Printed in U.S.A.

This book is dedicated to the thousands of volunteers who contribute their time, energy and expertise so integral to the heritage and ongoing success of the Conservancy of Southwest Florida.

CONTENTS

INTRODUCTION viii

An Early Inkling of Science 1
    Southwest Florida Experiments. 4

Malathion in the Morning. 12
    Rise of Chemicals 14
    Mosquito Control in South Florida 15
    Governor Graham Enters the Fray 19
    The Beat Goes On 20

Sea Turtle Projects 22
    Southwest Florida's Sea Turtles 24
    Early Research Efforts 27
    The Kemp's Ridley 30
    Future of Sea Turtles. 33
    Impact of Global Warming. 36

Walking Trees 38
    Florida's Mangroves 40
    Clam Bay. 42
    Mangrove Research 44

Pythons 47
    Origins. 48
    Morphology. 50

>   Into the U.S. 53
>   CISMA 53
>   Removal 55
>   Future 56

Policy 58

Rural Lands Stewardship Area 62

>   Blessed by the State 69
>   Ave Maria 70
>   Opening the Eastern Lands of the
>   Western Everglades 72
>   A New Look at Growth Management—
>   The Restudy 75
>   Enter Thaddeus Cohen 80
>   Town of Big Cypress 85
>   Rivergrass, Bellmar, and Longwater 86
>   Lawsuit Against Rivergrass 91
>   A Bit of History 93
>   Theory of the Case 95
>   Florida Panther 96
>   Housing Diversity 96
>   Fiscal Neutrality 97
>   In the Courts 98
>   The Appeal 101
>   Hyde Park Village 105
>   Immokalee Road Rural Village 106

v

Lee County and CREW 110
Corkscrew Road Builds Up 112

DR/GR 115
Getting Rid of Map 14 118
Cumulative Impacts 119
Saga of the Troyer Mine 119
Sakata Farms 122
Displacing the Panther 123
Corkscrew Swamp Sanctuary 123
Florida Farms Development 125
Kingston 126
All Together Now 130

404 Program 132
Objections by Earthjustice and the Conservancy 134
FDEP "Fesses Up" 142
The Sackett Case 144
Florida Calls the Shots 146

The Coast and the Corps 148
Ian 150
The Conservancy Takes the Lead 153
The Cost-Benefit Analysis 155
A Multi-county Strategy 158
One Final Stinky Problem 159
Nature-based Solutions 160

Care for Sick and Injured Wildlife 163
The Numbers 167
Knowing the Environment 168
Level of Support 168
Future 169

Education 172
School Programs 172
Adult Discovery..................................... 176
Education Prevails 178

Beyond the Pale 180

Orchids, Oil, and Airports 183
Home of the Ghost.................................. 184
Drill Baby Drill in the Big Cypress 185
Naples Airport in the Picayune Strand 191
Midnight Raid on Conservation Collier............. 194
Redux... 195

Final Thoughts at 60.................................. 197

ENDNOTES 202
INDEX 210
ACKNOWLEDGEMENTS 215

INTRODUCTION

Objections to a road along the outer barrier islands from Naples to Isles of Capri brought about the birth of the Conservancy of Southwest Florida. It moved from land acquisition, as a local chapter of the national Nature Conservancy, into an independent regional organization. Choices were always there to be made but education and science, as the basis for decisions to preserve the highest level of biodiversity and natural resources throughout southwest Florida, became central to its mission and continue to this day.

This book is a celebration of the 60th anniversary of the Conservancy. The story does not end in 2024 but brings to a close a decade of more game-changing decisions and challenges to the environment than any other in recent history, decisions about where and how growth should take place, about how to deal with an invasive reptile eating its way through the Everglades, Big Cypress and Fakahatchee, about how to protect a vast natural landscape with miles upon miles of coastal beaches, about how to value the importance of mangrove forests to nature's productivity and shoreline conservation, and to maintain the long-term viability of sea turtle nesting areas on barrier island beaches.

The science section begins with two little told stories from the 1960s and 1970s when the Conservancy undertook its first applied science project—to save and restore a declining population of one of Florida's great game fish—the snook. It then moves to a story of how mosquito control, to make life more livable in south Florida, had unintended consequences on the game fish population and how the Conservancy dealt with it. The purpose is to show how the early founders moved quickly beyond land acquisition and into the use of applied science to generate policy solutions to a problem they were concerned with and one of the reasons they moved to Naples in the first place.

Then, the Conservancy began to separate some of the science from building policy positions. The first example of this shift was how Conservancy scientists initiated regularly updated field studies on sea turtle nesting and foraging research, now one of the old data sets in the United States. The narrative moves along to research on the importance and viability of mangrove forests as coastal nurseries as well as nature's way to mitigate storm damage. Finally, it turns to the tale of the exotic Burmese python. It traces the origins of the snakes and their relentless population growth as they eat their way from Miami to Fort Myers.

The next set of chapters covers policy initiatives beginning with development in the eastern lands of Collier County. The story really began in 2002 but picked up steam until 2020 when the Conservancy filed one of the most expensive and difficult lawsuits in its history. It then chronicles the Conservancy's advocacy pressing against inappropriate development in the Density Reduction/ Groundwater Recharge area in Lee County that threatens one of south Florida's great places.

Development in Lee and Collier County went into overdrive with a messy transfer of Sec. 404 wetland destruction permitting from the federal government to the State of Florida. Conceived hastily and pushed through in the dying moments of the Trump Administration in 2020, it was known as the "Holy Grail" to the development community, and the Conservancy and its partners continued to point to the gaping holes left in the new iteration.

The policy section then turns to coastal storm resilience management and the role of the Conservancy played in slowing down a process pushed by the U.S. Army Corps of Engineers following Hurricane Ian that would have hardened Collier County's coast with structural seawalls.

The third section of the book is about the opening in 2012 of the largest animal and bird rescue recovery facility in southwest Florida and how the new facility has been able to handle a variety of patients, about the Conservancy's broad educational outreach using a mobile classroom and comprehensive curriculum in multiple venues, and about the opening of a new Discovery Center manned by dozens of volunteers. The education programs, like the wildlife facility, had a long history with the Conservancy but during the past decade were clearly affected by the outbreak of the COVID pandemic, and despite a brief interruption continued to adapt to the need to press forward in serving and educating.

Having thrived for 60 years, the Conservancy has never faced growth and population pressures at the amplified level that is now taking place, so the book will conclude with a number of observations and thoughts about the future from its chief executive for the past decade, Rob Moher. When asked to summarize his thoughts on the past ten years, he had this to say: "The history of the Conservancy covers a lot of ground. We have fantastic data sets on sea turtles and pythons. We know a lot about wetlands. We have studied the importance of mangroves for years. We have one of the most important animal and avian recovery facilities in South Florida and we have some superb exhibits and educational programs. But that's not really what it's about. The most important thing we have is our independence. We are not informed or influenced by anything other than our mission. We remain completely dedicated to the preservation of our land, water, and wildlife driven by science and nature-based solutions."

A DECADE IN REVIEW

An Early Inkling of Science

Kenneth Woodburn stood in front of the Collier County Planning Commission on a warm afternoon in late April 1967. On a display board was a large map showing a dotted line running from Marco Island for twenty miles south toward Carnestown representing a scenic drive cutting through the heart of coastal mangrove forests and snaking down a series of small barrier islands. The planning body was prepared to urge adoption of the map as part of the county's comprehensive plan. While the scheme was initially presented as an amenity for visitors, county planners added off-handedly that two-thirds of the periphery of the highway would be set aside for development, a formula common throughout Florida at the time.

Woodburn was appearing on behalf of the Collier County Conservancy, originally organized in 1964 to stop a "road to nowhere" from Naples to Marco Island. His appearance in 1967 was a sign that the Conservancy, once an outpost of resistance to wanton destruction of the mangrove fringe forests, was now becoming a *force majeure* when transportation planners undertook another attempt to build a combination of roads and causeways through what is now the heart of the Ten Thousand Islands.

Woodburn was, at the time, a marine biologist with the Board of Conservation, founded in 1933 to license salt water fishing boats.[1] Born in Pennsylvania in 1926, he had moved to Florida with his family when he was fifteen years old. With an academic background in tropical and subtropical biology, his entire career had been spent on water quality issues. Having done studies in Rookery Bay in 1964, he would later go to the Florida Fresh Water Fish and Game Commission (FWFGC) and then into Gov. Reubin Askew's inner circle in 1971 when Nathaniel Reed, leaving Tallahassee for Washington, suggested to Askew that he should appoint a close advisor on conservation issues. He filled the bill.

In his presentation, Woodburn was brief and to the point, concluding with this comment: "Naples and fishing, like love and marriage, go together. It is possible to have one without the other, but it is better with both. Fishing brings forty per cent of the people here. Many of them to catch snook, next to pompano, the most delicate Florida fish."[2]

The "most delicate" fish that Woodburn lauded in his comment to the planning body was the common snook, *Centropomus undecimalis,* one of southwest Florida's great game fish.[3] On the business end of a rod, it was anything but delicate. Growing to forty pounds, and capable of tail-walking leaps when hooked, the snook was a smaller version of the tarpon but was suffering from effects of dredges plying the coast and other indignities driven by human expansion into the wilds of south Florida. A river transient fish, it spawns during warmer months in deep holes within intertidal passes and in scour channels off beaches. Spawning occurs daily but becomes most active during the new and full phases of the moon. Each female is capable of producing over one million eggs which develop into the larval phase within two to three weeks. Larvae drift with the currents until they develop into maneuverable small juveniles. As soon as they are able, they head for creeks and backwater coastal areas where red mangrove roots provide shade, cover and nutrients for them, so with the decimation of mangrove fringes along southwest Florida's coast, habitat was slowly shrinking.

The snook, like many fish, can change sex from male to female. They leave the protection of the backwaters when they reach maturity, but research shows they tend to stay close to their natal beaches. Sex reversal takes place during the latter stages of a snook's life over a period of 60 to 90 days. There is no good scientific study that fully explains either the stimulus or process for this reversal, but by observation all the largest fish tend to be females.

Man alone was not the only cause of population decline. Snook are highly temperature sensitive. When the Gulf of Mexico falls below 60 Fahrenheit, snook become sluggish. If the temperature falls below that, or has dropped rapidly, they die. For example, an extreme cold snap in 2010, when water temperatures reached 56 Fahrenheit, killed over one million snook in the waters off Florida.

Southwest Florida Experiments

The first signs of collapse of the snook population were evident in the 1950s. The species was being heavily harvested commercially, but in 1957 the State of Florida made it illegal to take the fish by any means other than hook and line. Despite this drastic change in policy, the population continued a slow decline for the next decade. This was not lost on board members of the Collier County Conservancy, beginning with Charles Draper, a dedicated sport fisherman, who knew from his time on the water that the snook was in tough shape.

Draper was the first chairman and (unpaid) president of the Conservancy. Elected at its founding in 1964, he was a tall, lean former Air Force officer possessed of formidable organizing skills as long as it remained within the command-and-control management style to which he was accustomed. A man of few words who preferred others jump into the spotlight, he did not "suffer fools lightly." But he had no time to work on the snook problem. Memos from that era indicate a growing frustration with the lack of state intervention, but Draper decided to put his formidable energy into saving as much of Rookery Bay as he could during his three-year term as president.

Draper passed away at his summer home in Kennebunkport, Maine, in November of 1967 and the team he had recruited to succeed him was looking at a broader future for the Conservancy—a future beyond straight-up land acquisition. The organization was wrestling with the need to educate southwest Florida residents and visitors in the importance of maintaining the ecosystems so carefully prized into public ownership.

This was an important moment because Naples, at the time, was a quiet backwater in the early throes of development. For years, a visible abundance of seemingly inexhaustible natural resources gave rise to a sense that nature was the dominant force, able to renourish itself and to repair small blemishes inflicted by dredge-and-fill going on in the mangrove forests.

Southwest Florida was a rapidly growing coastal area with an essentially rural mentality and if the state was going to ignore burgeoning issues in the 1960s and early 1970s, Collier County would have to take them up, but the county commission's appointed Coastal Area Planning Advisory Committee was slow to recognize the rapid rate of urbanization. There was no planning staff. That work was carried on by contracted consultants, many of whom had conflicted allegiances. Land use decisions were made on a case-by-case basis depending, to some extent, on personal relationships between landowner and elected officials. And big changes were taking place inland.

The Rosen brothers, from Baltimore, had purchased 112,000 acres of land west of the Big Cypress Swamp and north of the Tamiami Trail. A simple system of ditches was designed to drain the land with water flowing into the Ten Thousand Islands. It was destroying habitat and the sport fishing community was up in arms.

Pressure to do something grew. Prompted by anecdotal evidence from board members—comments recorded in meeting minutes—the organization established a Fishing Committee in 1973 under the guidance of directors Breaux Ballard, Bill Oberhelman and Elmer Wavering who financially supported the first project. This was *de rigeur*, for in the early days of the Conservancy directors had great latitude in selecting projects but were expected to foot the bill for work undertaken in pursuit of their interests. Fortunately, all could afford it.

The trio had been highly successful in business. Ballard hailed from an eponymously named county in Kentucky and was a Princeton graduate with a variety of business holdings in his home state. Oberhelman, a Cincinnati native, started the Naples Community Foundation in 1985 with an initial endowment of $300,000 and became its first executive director. Wavering was a self-described "tinkerer," who with Bill Lear (founder of the Lear Jet Corporation) invented both the car radio and the auto alternator. Later ascending to the presidency of Motorola, Inc., he retired to Naples in 1972 where he became one of the leaders of the Conservancy.

The initial research project continued for four years from 1975 until 1979 and resulted in the tagging of 6,000 fish. Over 800 tags were returned, most taken within ten miles of the release point. The state's Department of Natural Resources (DNR) was able to extrapolate population and mortality estimates as well as movement and growth patterns from this data. At the same time, the FWFGC was examining the feasibility of artificial propagation for freshwater stocking. Since juvenile snook showed an affinity for fresh water, experiments were carried out to determine optimal conditions for fertilizing and distributing fry.[4] The Conservancy's committee jumped on the study as a possible solution to the crisis in the Gulf, only to be informed that the study was for fresh water inland lakes only and that "stocking of artificially cultivated fry into natural salt waters would be a total waste of money, time and effort."[5] This did little to chill Conservancy directors who pressed their case and the following year were offered some encouragement from the head of the state's Bureau of Marine Science and Technology: "I agree that snook may be reared from the egg to a juvenile size where they will survive in the wild."[6] This turnabout came about partly as a result of pressure from Ogden Phipps, a wealthy Miami sportsman who was chairman of the Fresh Water Fish and Game Commission at the time.

The Rookery Bay lab was given orders and enough money to begin work on a hatchery program. It managed to artificially hatch 600 snook in 1979 to one-inch size. After three years of trial-and-error experimentation, the scientists determined temperature was the main variable in successful propagation. By February, 1980, the

Conservancy represented by board members Breaux Ballard and Mary Dearholt, met with FWFGC staff in Tallahassee to discuss extending the hatching project. They expressed the organization's desire to proceed with an experimental stocking program beginning in freshwater canals, but commission staff balked insisting that millions of fry would be required to have any measurable impact on the overall population due to high predation. The Conservancy made one more try and, in the summer of 1980, managed to raise only 1,125 fingerlings—well below the needed number.

The Conservancy's interest in larval snook research then died off for five years, but returned in 1985 with the reinvigorated leadership of James Kessler, chairman of the newly christened Fisheries Resources Committee, who pledged to raise $58,000 for the University of Miami's snook research program with one *quid pro quo*: that juveniles in massive numbers be released into waters off Collier County. Kessler, who later became chairman of the Conservancy's board, was a devoted fisherman spending his summers on streams in Montana and winters in Marco Island so he could be a few minutes by boat from his beloved Ten Thousand Islands. The project was staffed by Ed Johanson, Advanced Projects Director for the Conservancy, also an avid fisherman and snook expert. The program managed to collect $60,200 in 1985 with over two hundred small gifts from $5 up, including 200 shares of Exxon Corporation stock worth $10,750 from Bill Allyn and a $5,000 check from the Norris Foundation established by Dellora and Lester Norris.

The program was launched with great fanfare. Large male and female snook were netted during the spawning season beginning in early May. The team from Miami went out only on the new and full moon. One night's log from June 1986 is typical of the hit-or-miss nature of the nighttime forays: "On Saturday morning Whitley Ward and Ed Johanson started fishing Gordon Pass. At 0500 Whitley caught a large female, 25 pounds. She was put in the tank and fishing resumed, without any further luck. Saturday during the day Todd Geroy fished but did not find any keepers. Sunday evening Jimbo fished from 1600 to 2200 (in the rain) and caught three—all too small. Thus the weekend ended with one lonely female in the tank and no appropriate suitors."[7]

It continued for two years, but Kessler and Johanson became convinced that the problem was compounded by loss of habitat and food sources for juvenile fish—a problem the Conservancy had been addressing with its land conservation efforts. The university's experimental fish hatchery released one million larval snook and 200 fingerlings into Collier County coastal waters in 1985 but as predicted it had little impact on the overall population. The mortality rate for released small fish was off the charts. Ed Johanson was aware that the snook population in Everglades National Park, which had little pollution (other than phosphorous and nitrogen), had crashed in the 1970s which he attributed to construction of a series of weirs which prevented juveniles from seeking refuge into the brackish backwaters of the park. He knew that fingerlings sought the estuarine niche between fresh and salt water, and concluded that the growth in drainage canals and construction of weirs had altered the balance of nature sufficiently to deprive smaller fish of the ability to move into the backwaters where salt water predators found the water too brackish. These findings never affected water management practices because control of systems went through the Army Corps of Engineers and water management districts. Local governments generally deferred to those two entities—both of which cared little about what appeared on the business end of someone's fishing rod.

The project ended with less of a bang and more of a whimper. "Enclosed is a check for $500 for snook tags. Hope this will keep things afloat for a while. When you get a chance, we would appreciate receiving some summary data on what you have been able to piece together on the Naples snook puzzle for the last 11 years."[8]

The snook program, standing alone, was not successful in finding a way to increase the population without resorting to other measures such as changes in catch limits and closing the season during certain months. Despite its failure, the project marked formation of a natural and mutually beneficial alliance between the Conservancy, Florida Department of Natural Resources fishery staff and the sport fishing community. That relationship continues to this day with the annual Red Snook Fishing Tournament, raising substantial funds for continuing research and habitat preservation. It was a demonstration of the value of applied science, as opposed to pure research, in dealing with one of Florida's treasured natural resources—"the most delicate Florida fish."

By 1987, scientists at the Conservancy and the university confirmed that adding high levels of pesticides from mosquito control spraying were suppressing crustaceans in the vulnerable larval stage. This was a critical link in the food chain for juvenile snook, with the result that few of the released snook were growing to spawning age. It was the basis for the Conservancy's next foray into applied science—the issue of mosquito control and unintended consequences.

Malathion in the Morning

On the west coast of Florida there are about three dozen varieties of mosquitoes. Most common is the salt marsh mosquito—*Aedes taenioihynchus*—which reproduces year-round in intertidal mud flats, swamps, and marshes. It is widely dispersed from Massachusetts to the Caribbean and can travel up to 100 miles. Females bite, needing blood to produce eggs. Prey is detected by a combination of chemical signals, radiation emitted in the infrared and sight. The insect's saliva prevents clotting and creates the itching sensation that accompanies a mosquito bite. The salt marsh mosquito does not depend heavily, as do some of its cousins, upon rainfall to create egg-laying environments.

Other species begin to appear in what Andrew Jackson called the "sickly season." When Jackson's troops fought two wars against Seminole tribes in Florida, accounts were written by men desperate to remove themselves from the ubiquitous "swamp angels" invading their eyes, ears, mouth, and nasal passages in massive swarms sometimes smothering the soldiers' sensory organs. While it was rumored that some soldiers shot themselves after being driven to near-madness by the biting insects, Native

Americans—the Seminoles—had found two ways to cope with the problem. The first involved boiling gar and other fatty fish, and coating their bodies with oily residue. The second method employed smudge pots, slow burning and smoky, but neither worked as well as a stiff breeze.

Another genus is *Anopheles,* familiar to many as the main carrier of malaria. While it is impossible to ignore the problem of disease vectors, the mosquito serves a number of useful purposes. It pollinates plants. In the larval stage, it is a major food source for small fish particularly in the backwaters of South Florida's mangrove forests.

Anopheles also serves as the primary food source for the dragonfly. Better known as the "skeeterhawk," the dragonfly has an eye structure that allows it to see nearly everywhere except behind its head. Flying up to five miles a day, it is able to operate aerially much like a helicopter, moving forward and backward while rising vertically. The dragonfly feeds only when it is airborne by catching mosquitoes in basket-shaped legs. It can consume up to a hundred mosquitoes in one day (depending upon the size of the mosquitoes).

A number of other predators use the mosquito as a dietary supplement (but not a staple). The purple martin, popularly regarded as a classic controller, generally flies too high to find the low altitude mosquito searching for protein in the form of animal blood. Bats are slightly better, but they prefer larger meals such as moths that provide more nourishment for less effort—a tactic known as optimal foraging strategy.[9]

Rise of Chemicals

While many people prefer control methods within nature's existing structure, the earliest attempts to chemically control mosquitoes called for massive amounts of oil to be poured into drainage ditches where the ubiquitous pests reproduced at warp speed. The idea was helpful but limited in its effect. Then, in 1945, DDT—dichlorodiphenyltrichloroethane—came upon the scene. It had been invented by a German scientist in 1874 but was not widely used until the Second World War when it was used to destroy head lice in prisoners and refugees.

DDT not only killed head lice, but it also killed cockroaches, ants, bees, flies, beetles, moths, caterpillars, bedbugs and, of course, mosquitoes—until they adapted. Mutating into resistant species, more and more DDT was required to kill off the little devils until people in Florida began to notice that the bird population was in decline.

While it was initially effective, the widespread use of DDT enraged a meticulous scientist named Rachel Carson. A carefully documented analysis of the effect of DDT on birds, particularly eagles and Peregrine Falcon, led to the banning of DDT in the United States in 1972. The decision was not complicated. After peaking in 1960, use of the chemical declined as insects began to develop resistance to its effects, occurring when those mosquitoes that were able to reproduce passed along the ability to resist to the next generation.

Mosquito Control in South Florida

There are two means of chemically killing mosquitoes: larvaciding and adulticiding. Larvaciding was tried first using aerial or truck spraying to apply an oily application of chemicals to wet areas where larvae were found. Adulticiding was later carried out by vaporizing insecticides into a fine mist or fog and floating it through the free-flying population. A newer method of adulticiding, called ultra-low volume (ULV) spraying, uses highly concentrated chemicals forced through nozzles at high speed and disseminated by either aircraft or spray trucks.

While door and window screens made life inside a house more pleasant, chemical mosquito control in Collier County began in 1950 in the City of Naples. The Naples Mosquito Control District (NMCD) was given ad valorem taxing powers, overseen by three elected commissioners and no money to begin with so the city fathers financed a truck and driver in 1951 to begin spraying. The truck was known as "Smoky Joe." It was chased merrily along city streets by dozens of kids running in and out of the mist which was a combination of diesel oil and Malathion.

Malathion is an organic phosphate. When first compared to DDT, a chlorinated hydrocarbon, it was deemed to be safe. Widely used in gardens and households, it was metabolized and broken down by enzymes in the human liver. Then, the Food and Drug Administration found that while Malathion alone was harmless, when paired with other organic phosphates it was deadly. And the two did not have to be ingested or absorbed simultaneously; the use of one within a week had the potential to inhibit the detoxifying liver enzyme. The NMCD used Malathion on a regular basis until the supply ran out, due to increased demand for insecticides throughout the Southeastern United States with its rapidly growing population.

By 1982, the district had changed its name to the Collier Mosquito Control District (CMCD), reflecting an added two hundred square miles of coverage. The district's boundary was clearly defined and generally limited to the most populous areas but was surrounded by salt marshes and mangrove forests—all hospitable to the little biting, flying pests seeking protein for their egg-laying. And much of that fringe area lay within the Rookery Bay Aquatic Reserve, saved by efforts of the Conservancy and owned by the State of Florida.

The CMCD stepped up its larvaciding efforts in the 1980s. Over the span of several years, it was proven that the large-scale larvaciding did not decrease the need for adulticiding "... because of the migration of salt marsh mosquitoes [into populated areas], aerial adulticiding remains the primary control method." [10]

But it had another outcome. Gerald Bruger, a biologist with the Florida Department of Natural Resources (DNR), studying snook in the Ten Thousand Islands, documented a 70% population decline.[11] The Conservancy's board, many of whom were fishermen, were supportive. The department's confidential request to limit spraying during the spawning season was met with a brusque rebuff by CMCD director Brandt Watson: "My mandate is controlling mosquitoes." [12] With the tacit support of the Conservancy, pressure was brought on the local district by Elton Gissendanner, director of DNR and an old friend who had fought hard for state purchase of Cannon Island in Rookery Bay and against creation of Villages of Sabal Bay, a massive Collier Development Corporation project that threatened to destroy mangrove fringe along Naples Bay and ended up in the courts for thirteen years.

The controversy was rapidly developing legs and at the center it was Gissendanner. He was convinced that his naturalist, Bruger, had it right. The snook population was being decimated by either careless or uncaring local officials, and while DNR lacked the power to halt the use of a toxin called Baytex, he was determined to put a stop to it. The Conservancy was aware of the magnitude of the problem but stayed on the sidelines for fear of alienating large numbers of people who relied upon mosquito control to live in southwest Florida.

By January 1985, *Florida Sportsman* magazine ran a long article on the issue pointing out that Collier County; having used 97,288 pounds of poisons in 1980 had upped the ante to 159,000 pounds in 1984. By comparison, the entire State of California had used a little over 70,000 pounds in 1980. It cited the work of Bruger at DNR, who had discovered seven miles of dead sand fleas along Collier County beaches after a CMCD aircraft sprayed over the Gulf of Mexico.

Burger's supposition was the decline in snook population was due to the mosquito larvae toxin settling into the shallow water estuaries along the coast. He received studies done in June and December of 1976 at Sanibel Island and another from 1981 in Rookery Bay which concluded that "the calculated application rates of Baytex and malathion presently used for mosquito control are lethal to the eggs and larvae of snook." [13]

With the gauntlet thrown down, pilots went quickly to work until Collier County Audubon Society asked the CMCD to stop spraying Coconut Island, at Big Marco and Capri Pass, the main channels into Collier Creek. The district's aircraft had sprayed the site of an active bald eagle's nest with Baytex three times during the month of May and the bald eagle, at the time, was on the federal "endangered species" list.

The local Audubon chapter complained bitterly that the spraying was going to kill the nesting pair of birds. "Coconut Island is a delicate wetlands area," wrote Pat Ware of Audubon, "and should not have been sprayed. This action reflects your insensitivity to local environmental matters, as well as to the fate of our national bird." Brandt Watson responded: "We've been using it since the '60s and there's a considerable number of birds around." [14] His acidic comment may have reflected his opinion of environmental organizations, because he failed to mention that he had already agreed to stop spraying the island at the request of the Florida Game and Freshwater Fish Commission.

The chemical of choice, Baytex, was another organophosphate known generically as fenthion. Audubon was correct in its distaste for the compound; in one formulation it was called "Rid-a-Bird." Developed in 1960 by Bayer, it was widely used in Europe as an avicide.[15] The American Bird Conservancy and Audubon were in full pursuit of the product, which was decimating the piping plover along Florida's beaches. The Piping plover, with its short bill, orange legs and black ring around its neck, was listed as "protected" under the Endangered Species Act in 1986 after being hunted to extinction by the end of the 19th century. Current estimates place the mating pair population at around 1,400. Fenthion, applied through ULV aerial spraying, was killing the little birds both on contact and from inhalation and was highly toxic to aquatic invertebrates—a major food source for the plover. It also acted as a stomach insecticide so the raptorial eagle was in jeopardy after consuming fenthion-exposed prey. The potent substance was later pulled from the market after its effects on non-target species was proven.[16]

Governor Graham Enters the Fray

By this time, insecticide spraying had become an issue throughout the state. Gov. Bob Graham convened a working group representing three mosquito control district directors, officials from the health and environmental protection agencies of the state and federal governments and faculty from the University of Florida to study the effects of aerial adulticiding on coastal habitats and inhabitants.

The group was beset by controversy from the first meeting. A number of workshops were held throughout the state in 1985. Collier County, through a citizen's organization called Citizen F.A.C.T.S. (an acronym For Alternative Controls to Toxic Sprays) had been formed in 1983 to disseminate information about the mosquito control district's activities—pointing out that the CMCD used more pounds of pesticides in one year than the entire State of California.

Final regulations went into effect in 1987. Spraying was restricted to instances where there was a clear, demonstrated need based upon mosquito counts and the possibility of a disease outbreak. The rules relied heavily upon the use of mosquito traps to estimate the pestiferous population, and upon anecdotal observation by licensed personnel. Aerial adulticide spraying of shorelines was permitted only when the trap count increased three-fold.

The Beat Goes On

The era of spraying by necessity was ushered in by a cooperative undertaking between the CMCD and Dave Addison, a scientist at the Conservancy funded by the Department of Health and Rehabilitative Services. Up to that point, the Conservancy had been a participant in the process; now it began to emerge as a force. The chief scientist, Mark Benedict, had been in the job for two years. He was determined to set some of the science effort apart from policy decisions but had his hands full. The Conservancy had also been pulled into a controversy about the dredging of Gordon Pass, setting the supportive Gaynor family, descendants of Dellora and Lester Norris, against the obdurate Benedict who was trying to keep the science department out of the fray.

Benedict's tenure at the Conservancy marked a transition. Early projects like the snook study were undertaken in support of a specific goal using applied science. With no university in southwest Florida and an unusual ecosystem beginning to be stressed, he felt that pure research—the quest for knowledge—was worth the time and effort. There would be occasional interstices where science and policy initiatives would interact but the trajectory was clear. The work would be straightforward, peer-reviewed and done by scientists.

To do that, he had Dave Addison who was undertaking one of the most durable scientific research projects in the world—creation of baseline data on sea turtle nesting.

Sea Turtle Projects

Sitting on the Conservancy's deck in late January 2014, the weather was unusually warm. Dave Addison was pondering my question: "Why do you think sea turtles hold such great appeal for people? Is it the eyes?"

"No," he said, "I don't think it's the eyes. Sea turtles do have large eyes and people depend to a great extent on eye contact in their relationships, so the size of the eyes might be somehow related to accessibility. But I think more important, they are slow-moving, predictable and non-threatening so everyone, even small children can be near them with no fear of harm. That's important. They can't run away from humans like most wild critters. You're not going to approach a panther or raccoon, but the sea turtle... that's a different matter. Besides they can't pull into their shell like a box turtle, so they're easy for people to relate to." [17]

Addison, dressed in a T-shirt and cargo pants, has an "aw shucks" manner about him but beneath that casual exterior is a serious scientist, one of the foremost experts in the United States and guiding light for over three decades of one of the longest scientific undertakings in southwest

Florida: the Conservancy's renowned sea turtle nesting and monitoring project.

"Besides," he continued, "if you go back to prehistoric times, you'll find there was an emotional connection with turtles. I don't know why, but it's there."

Indeed it was there. Frank Hamilton Cushing, in his extraordinary find at Key Marco in 1896, uncovered a beaked turtle head painted black, blue, white and red that had been part of a larger wooden figure, likely ceremonial, dating back over a thousand years. The Calusa, a hegemonous tribe on Florida's southwest coast, used turtles in a ritual context. Burial mounds on islands in Charlotte harbor were guarded by effigies of turtles and barracuda "... whose function was to appease the dead."[18] A dietary staple of indigenous people, the Calusa, also used turtle bones as gauges to give their fishing nets uniform mesh sizes.[19]

In the late 1800s, corrals—known as kraals—were built in coastal waters off Key West to house turtles brought from the Caribbean. Others, as available, were locally caught and similarly impounded, to later make their way onto white tablecloths as steaks and soups—all part of the standard dining fare in the Keys. An article in *Harper's Weekly* in 1890 described the situation: "The habitués of North American restaurants and the aldermanic stomachs of London must needs be supplied with green turtle soup.... the demand for shell adornments, so dear and so necessary to the lady's boudoir, will be met...."[20] This practice continued until biologists, notably Dr. Archie Carr of the University of

Florida, brought attention to the rapid decline of the species and regulations to protect sea turtles were put in place. Carr was a renowned herpetologist beginning work in the 1930s and carrying through the late 1980s. He became one of the legendary figures in Florida's pantheon of natural scientists responsible, in part, for asking many of the questions about sea turtles that today's researchers, including Dave Addison, are attempting to answer.

Southwest Florida's Sea Turtles

Sea turtles are among the oldest surviving species on the planet. They have been around, essentially unchanged, for over 150 million years, surviving the Cretaceous era collapse that did the dinosaurs in. Highly adapted to an aqueous environment, the reptiles possess powerful flippers that make them strong swimmers and allow them to dive deep for prey. The forward flippers are elongated and provide propulsion while the hind flippers basically serve as a rudder and to elevate the turtle in the water column. There is also a theory that the evolutionary success of sea turtles is related to their "armored tank" adaptation giving up anatomical flexibility for protection.[21]

There are five varieties of sea turtles nesting in southwest Florida. The most abundant is the loggerhead, growing to an adult size of 3' and weighing up to 300 pounds. Easily identified by its block-shaped head, housing jaws with tremendous crushing power, they thrive on a diet of shellfish and crustaceans. Listed as "threatened" in

1978, the population has been stable for last two decades partly because in 1989, shrimpers in the Gulf of Mexico were required to install turtle excluder devices (TED) in their nets, similar to trap doors, to allow turtles to escape seining.

The green sea turtle is larger than the loggerhead, growing to 5' but weighing about the same. These herbivorous reptiles are listed as "endangered," and nest in limited numbers in the Florida Keys and Florida Bay, but by 1994 a few nests showed up sporadically on Key Island. Both species were prized: "... the eggs of the green sea turtle are larger than those of the loggerhead, and are palatable by epicures. The superiority of flavor is supposed to be due to their food, which is chiefly vegetable." [22]

The leatherback is the Sumo wrestler of the species. Listed as "endangered" in 1970, they sometimes exceed 7' in length. Behemoths of the ocean, they can weigh up to 1,500 pounds, gained primarily with the jellyfish as their dietary staple. Jellyfish are mostly water, but what the turtles lose in calories they make up in quantity; juvenile leatherbacks can eat up to twice their weight daily of the gooey prey. Unfortunately, the ubiquitous white plastic grocery and garbage bag looks like a jellyfish in the water and poses an occasional threat to the species. The leatherback is named for its rubbery carapace which, insulated by an inch or two of fat, allows the "endangered" leatherback to migrate into frigid waters by adjusting their body temperature to survive. A very few nest along Florida's coast. Curiously, the leatherback escaped predation: "... the largest of all, the gigantic trunkback, frequently attaining a length of twelve feet and weighing a ton . . . is a flesh eater, and unwholesome, if not poisonous, to man."[23]

The last two species are the hawksbill and Kemp's ridley sea turtles. The hawksbill lives mainly in the Caribbean Sea. Slightly smaller than the loggerhead and fond of sponges for dinner, the hawksbill's carapace scutes are highly prized as ornamentation and jewelry. Bracelets, with streaks of black and brown on an amber background can be purchased in Havana, Cuba, but only after asking a merchant to display the illegally gotten baubles always hidden behind a curtain out of sight of the authorities in the open-air markets.

The Kemp's ridley is named after Richard Kemp, who first discovered the species off Key West in 1880. The discovery was noted as follows by Samuel Garman, assistant director of herpetology at Harvard's Museum of Comparative Zoology: ". . . about three years ago, Richard M. Kemp, of Florida, directed my attention to a peculiar turtle, commonly called the 'bastard,' found in the Gulf of Mexico and said to be a cross between the green and loggerhead. At a later date, he secured for the museum a pair of fine specimens, which furnished the material for a description given below. In consideration of the great interest Mr. Kemp takes in matters pertaining to natural history, it is most appropriate that the species he has been the means of bringing into notice should bear his name."[24]

Both species have been found in Estero Bay and Pine Island Sound off Lee County's shore and are studied closely by Conservancy scientists.

Early Research Efforts

The Conservancy began studying reproductive cycles of the reptiles in 1981, the year Lanny Sherwin, publisher of *Gulf Shore Life* magazine was elected as a new director. "He spent a lot of time out there on his dirt bike," said Addison. "He was kind of the father of the turtle work we did out there; when he got on the board he got interested in the turtles and then by '85 we were collecting data that was comparable over the years so there was consistency. That's important—getting the baseline set right—then everything that follows is meaningful."[25]

Sherwin then turned to an old friend of the Conservancy, Ross Obley, who was largely responsible for the environmental success of Pelican Bay. Obley, in turn, got the local Rotary Club to fund construction of a large wire hatchery to protect eggs from predation by raccoons on Key Island.[26] Wire mesh on the cages was sized so smaller hatchlings could crawl through on their way to the Gulf. In its first year, the hatchery protected over 1,300 of the relocated ping-pong ball-sized eggs and the program was on its way.

Key Island is the region's most productive hatchery location. In 1984, scientists began "Operation Headstart." As a test to ensure survival, 24 loggerheads and six green turtles (from Florida's east coast) were impounded in a large filtered recirculating sea water tank at the Conservancy's lab. Bacteria were disposed of with ultraviolet light, and the reluctant captives dined on bait fish and lettuce. When reaching a little over a pound in weight, they were then released as tagged yearlings onto the beaches at Key Island. 96% of the first year's cohort survived.[27]

A parallel project known as "Turtle Rescue" was begun in 1984 by Caretta Research, an independent non-profit. Concerned with human and four-legged interference in the nesting and hatching process, it recruited dozens of volunteers to go out at night, battling weather, mosquitoes and failing equipment, to monitor and protect southwest Florida beaches between Clearwater and Cape Sable. Over seven thousand eggs were counted in nests, and the protective activity successfully reduced mortality significantly. Over three thousand hatchlings successfully crawled into the warm Gulf waters by the first of August.

The following year the number of hatchlings topped nine thousand, a new record, and with the large number of little turtles, scientists had enough data to begin to draw some preliminary hypotheses about the survival efficacy of the sea turtle population. The Conservancy's Gary Schmelz and Ron Mezich determined that sexual differences in hatchlings varied by beach locations. Those areas with lower nest temperatures produced more males; warmer nests produced more females. The cause? Exotic causarina (or Australian pines), brought to Key Island for beach stabilization. Tall swaying trees produced lengthy shadows which lowered nest temperatures. Equally important, by observation the scientists determined that the Australian pine, a shallow-rooted tree, was a major impediment to females finding locations with enough soft sand in which to nest.

Then, Schmelz and Mezich noted that as renourishment of public beaches took place while tourists were enjoying cooler climes, female turtles tended to make more "false crawls" on new sand and build nests closer to the water, with significantly lower hatch rates due to the heavy machinery used during the renourishment process and mechanical raking for maintenance.

Collier County beaches from Wiggins to Gordon Pass are constructed for the benefit of tourists; there is nothing natural about them which is why sea turtles prefer the protected beaches of Key Island for summertime nesting. This issue of the remarkable ability of sea turtles to detect the color and grain size of sand on their natal beaches remains under continuing study. While tolerance for grain size is fairly broad, scientists believe nesting rejection most likely has to do with the texture of the sand (inconsistent due to mechanical renourishment), the shape of the beach, and compaction as a result of heavy vehicles traversing the sand.

Finally, the Conservancy's scientists and volunteers knew that residential and street lighting along the coast was becoming a problem. Nesting females tended to avoid areas with bright lights. Hatchlings, depending upon the night sky to guide them toward the water, become confused by inland light sources leading to higher mortality.[28]

As the Conservancy's research progressed, it became well-known throughout the world for both its longevity and purity of data. A number of doctoral dissertations have come out of the sea turtle tagging and research program. Dave Addison has put hundreds of interns through the program—many of whom have gone on to do great things. As he reflected on his career, sitting on the deck of the Conservancy, the passion came out: "The science was always good, but the best part is those kids and what it did for them."[29]

By the spring of 2005, the Conservancy celebrated twenty years of research with consistent data. Over 212,000 hatchlings had been protected which, with a conservative assumed survival rate of 1 per 1,000 translated into 212 productive adults, reaching maturity in 20-30 years and then having a reproductive cycle of another 30 years. The project continues to this day, making the Conservancy's data set one of the longest-running and most credible in sea turtle research worldwide while looking forward to 2025 to celebrate 40 years of superb data.

The Kemp's Ridley

The smallest of Florida's sea turtles, it forages throughout the coastal waters all the way around to southwest Florida. Now the rarest of the various species, Kemp's ridley was estimated to have no more than 500 nesting females, hanging on by a thread, one per cent of its 1947 population base when as many as 40,000 came ashore in a single day.[30] Its main nesting ground is on the Gulf coast of Mexico where rapacious harvesting over the years at the main nesting site at Rancho Nuevo, decimated the species. Recently, the Mexican government has taken steps to curb the (now illegal) taking of the Kemp's ridley adults and eggs resulting in temporary stabilization of the population.[31] The Kemp's ridley was also the driving force behind the excluder devices installed in fishing nets.

The Kemp's ridley is also the most enigmatic of the sea turtles. One, from the National Marine Fisheries Service Laboratory in Galveston, Texas, was released at Homosassa and found a year and a half later off the coast of France, probably after floating in the large Atlantic loop current. Fascinated by a species near extinction, it has been Jeff Schmid's main area of study since he was a graduate student working with a protégé of Archie Carr's named Larry Ogren studying the Kemp's ridley in a small community in north central Florida using fishermen as the primary source of information, then testing the folk wisdom against scientific reality. His conclusion: the fishermen knew a lot about the turtles and where to catch them, but he wanted to know more.

Schmid, now Environmental Research Manager, took a PhD degree from the University of Florida and began working at the Conservancy in 2000 and as an adjunct faculty member at Florida Gulf Coast University.

In one of his first projects, conducted with Mote Marine Laboratory, he was able to survey foraging habitat and strategies of a small number of captured Kemp's ridley in Charlotte Harbor and adjacent Gulf coastal waters with a grant funded by Florida's sea turtle license plate, the Save the Sea Turtle Foundation, and a number of Conservancy donors who—for the price of a transmitter—got to name the turtle. The project yielded useful data on movements in response to water temperature changes and diet—mainly tunicates and spider crabs—all helpful in determining management protocols to protect this most endangered of sea turtles highly concentrated in Gulf waters.

In 2008 he released a Kemp's ridley named Kyra (for his daughter) fitted with a satellite transmitter into Pine Island Sound to study the effect of water temperature on the turtle's foraging patterns. As the study expanded, he realized that there was a regular pattern to their movement, seasonal migration from southwest Florida up to Cedar Key then as weather fronts swept the Gulf back again as temperatures cooled.

One unanswered mystery is the absence of Kemp's ridley remains in the prehistoric shell middens of coastal Florida. The larger, and more abundant, loggerhead appears frequently, as does the green sea turtle, along with fish bones, manatee and other marine animal remains. But the Kemp's ridley is not there, leading to speculation that the species may have been regarded with suspicion by prehistoric people.

Future of Sea Turtles

Multiple sea turtle research projects around the world have brought the plight of these creatures into public awareness. The fascination lies not only in the appeal of the creatures, but also in the many questions that surround their mysterious life cycles. Where are the males when the females are nesting? That question is still unanswered.

What is their attraction to mud? In the mid-1980s, when the South Florida Water Management District and U.S. Army Corps of Engineers opened the floodgates of Lake Okeechobee, a massive quantity of water trashed the marine ecosystem off Palm Beach County and dumped up to three feet of mud over the coastal coral reefs. Divers noted, immediately after the event, that a large number of loggerheads had moved into the area—not seen there before—to burrow into the mud.

How turtles cope with blooms of red tide is another looming issue. *Karenia brevis*, the local dinoflagellate, exists as a naturally occurring part of the Gulf of Mexico's ecosystem. Starting offshore on the Florida Shelf, it periodically moves toward the land driven by warming waters in the Florida Loop Current and its gyres. With nutrients like trichodesmium widely available and an upwelling (onshore) wind as it approaches the land, it feeds on urban runoff. According to data compiled by the Florida Fish and Wildlife Conservation Commission, there were nearly 60 sporadic outbreaks between 1844 and 1995, but since then the blooms have become almost annual events in the late summer and fall off the coast.

Schmid is not convinced that all sea turtles are able to detect and avoid red tide. One of his transmitter-affixed turtles, named Dorothy, was a source of fascination as she moved in and out of Pine Island Sound while a large outbreak of red tide was lying offshore. Most sea turtles avoid red tide, but she swam out into the heart of the bloom with the inevitable result.

The pattern of individual sea turtle movements is another of the enigmas that fascinate scientists. Their main activity is foraging—looking for food. But how do the various species manage to cruise thousands of miles over a period of two or more years, and then return to their home beaches for nesting? According to research done by Dr. Joseph Kirschvinc at the California Institute of Technology Rock Magnetism Laboratory, one explanation is that sea turtles, like homing pigeons, porpoises and yellowfin tuna, possess millions of tiny, ferromagnetic crystals in their brains which they use to navigate. Research on loggerheads has shown that as they move to eventually find their way back to their natal beaches along the east coast of Florida, they swim between magnetic anomalies on the ocean floor. These humps of iron exert intense magnetic fields, many times stronger than the earth's background field and the data revealed that loggerheads keep to a course of minimal energy, while avoiding the deposits in the humps.

Loggerhead research at Woods Hole Laboratory in the 1970s found turtles moving from the Gulf north as far as New Jersey and New England, returning to Florida as the water cooled down.

This migratory behavior forms the basis for one plausible theory of the sea turtle's ability to locate home beaches. As a case on point, although not to specifically track the magnetic anomalies, Schmid tracked a turtle named Shelley from southwest Florida along the Gulf Coast all the way down to her natal beach in Mexico at Rancho Nuevo. After nesting she moved back north until her transmitter stopped in March 2017.

The nesting area at Rancho Nuevo has been highly protected since the 1970s and the Kemps ridley now has a chance of regaining its foothold within the Gulf of Mexico, in mute testament to stewardship of the coastal birthplace of these appealing creatures.

In the end, the greatest threat to sea turtles on remote beaches like Key Island is not the aquatic and beach habitat: it is on four legs. Mortality of eggs and hatchlings, believed in the 1980s to be around as high as 98 in 100, may be even as high as 999 in 1,000 according to current estimates. With each Kemp's ridley female laying as many as 300 eggs during the nesting season, up to 100 at a time, it requires an enormous effort to grow the population, especially when eggs are a staple of that ubiquitous night stalker, the common raccoon. As humans colonize more and more of southwest Florida, these predators are being pushed out of their native habitat, and the fellow with the striped tail is highly adapted to coexisting with people.

As Dave Addison put it: "With a long-lived animal like the turtle these data sets become more valuable over time. And then individual animals can start to tell you their stories. You can talk to the animals; they just don't speak the way you think they're gonna speak, but the message is we need to get along a little better and do some things on a global basis that are more constructive than what we've been doing."[32]

Impact of Global Warming

Jeff Schmid is cautious in speculating about the effect of global warming and climate change on the population. "I think it will probably change migrating behavior. It may change the incubation outcome as well since warmer sand will produce more females, but it's interesting that in our research on Key Island the population of hatchlings is about 50-50 male and female. Bottom line: there are lots of moving parts."

"I think the weather short-term is also interesting in the effect it has on the diet of the turtles. We did a study in 2004 and found that the normal diet of tunicates had shifted and the turtles were eating sponges. After hurricane Irma, we found that they were eating blue crabs rather than spider crabs and then they turned back to tunicates. I would guess that the availability of prey was the determining variable and if there were pathogens destroying or modifying their diet the turtles would downshift their menu preferences."

Schmid is soft-spoken and chooses his words carefully. He has affixed transmitters and tracked nearly 60 turtles, but when asked about his work over the past 36 or more years he was characteristically modest. "We tried to save the Kemp's ridley from the extinction and I think we did. In 1986 we simply didn't know much about them, about how they live, what they eat and how they move back and forth in the Gulf. We didn't know how various environmental factors play into the decline of the population. So what I've done really is fill in the pieces. I still have a lot of data that needs to be put together and published for review but I think we are making progress as the success of the nesting seasons at Rancho Nuevo shows."

"I also think all this goes to show what resiliency they have. After all they have survived for hundreds of millions of years. They are still here and if we take care of their environment for them—they will thrive."

Walking Trees

While the sea turtle program was running full steam, a second area of scientific inquiry was opened up on the role of mangroves in southwest Florida's coastal waters. It was an example of core scientific research projects initiated by the Conservancy that became a hallmark of the organization. Much of it was due to Mark Benedict and the capable staff he recruited. It placed the Conservancy in an elite category of organizations in a state where scientific research received scant attention and funding from the legislature until the 1990s when the University of Florida and Florida State University were recognized as two of the country's better public research universities. The University of Miami, a private university, developed an international reputation for its research capabilities by not having to rely heavily on public funding.

The Conservancy's work focused on southwest Florida which had no institution of higher learning until Florida Gulf Coast University was chartered, so it filled a much-needed niche on species and habitat that no other organization in the region could approach as effectively and comprehensively with the exception of the Sanibel-Captiva Conservation Association in Lee County.

There were occasional interstices where pure science of necessity was applied as with the die-off of dozens of acres of black mangroves in Clam Bay. Conservancy scientists had been emphasizing the commercial connection between the value of estuaries and mangrove fringes and sustainability of the fishing industry for years, believing the economic argument was the mainspring for public and legislative support.

The Conservancy's landmark Naples Bay study in 1975 had paid scant attention to mangrove forests surrounding the bay; it was more concerned with water quality and benthic habitat. Studies conducted during the 1970s and 1980s dealing with species propagation began to emphasize the importance of mixed red mangrove root systems as a nursery for small fish. Most studies were done in Everglades National Park until mangrove research become critical in 1991 when a massive black mangrove die off began in the northern part of the Clam Bay Natural Resource Protection Area.

The cause was hydrological alteration to the bay causing pneumatophores to "drown." The situation worsened over the years and in 1999 Pelican Bay Foundation decided to ask Collier County to prevent total inundation during the wet season by improving drainage in the upper bay. It also engaged Steve Bortone, head of the Environmental Science Department, who initiated mangrove studies in 2000 by commenting in a report to the board "the mangrove forest is the predominant climax community yet little is known about its function, response to stress, and restoration."[33] A young scientist named Kathy Worley published a paper on the subject in 2005 using the Clam Bay experience as a scientific analog for similar restoration efforts worldwide. [34] She had begun her mangrove assessments by working with Bortone, had co-directed the sea turtle monitoring project at the same time with David Addison, and succeeded him as Director of Environmental Science.

Florida's Mangroves

Florida's Gulf Coast is populated by mangroves, a tree adapted to fluctuating salinity and water levels in the intertidal zone. They are able to deal with disabling soils, but have to establish themselves above the mean low tide level and can tolerate areas where it dries out during the dry season.

The mangrove swamps of south Florida are a dynamic and viscous environment of nutrient-laden detritus renourished continuously from the trees and from sediment trapped by the widespread root systems as water moves in and out. The rich soup has places to hide from predators and is a perfect nursery for small fish, shrimp, crab, snails and young turtles. With the protective cover, mangroves are highly suited as bird rookeries with the result that a high level of droppings add to the nutrient rich environment in which the trees grow.

There are four separate species. The red mangrove is generally along the outer areas of the coast, tolerant of submersion with stilt-like roots that brace the tree against tidal action giving it the nickname of the "walking tree." The taproots are not deep but spread widely along the horizontal access to anchor them during powerful windstorms. The red mangrove excretes salt with a filtration system at the surface of its roots. They grow to be as high as 80 feet with a circumference of the trunk of nearly 7 feet.

Moving closer inland is the black mangrove. It requires aeration of its roots allowing it to pass oxygen and carbon dioxide in and out of its root system through vertical poles known as pneumatophores. Unlike the red, the black mangrove excretes salt on the underside of its leaves and can grow as high as 60 feet generally in marsh habitats that flood infrequently.

The white mangrove, the most inland of the three, also excretes salt and has a similar need for aeration of the root system and occupies even higher ground. The fourth, known as button–mangrove, is technically not part of the species but grows near the others, so is sometimes included in the successional forest.

Red mangroves have propagules that look like inverted pencils when they float into the intertidal areas having been dropped as seedlings from the trees. They attach themselves to oyster reefs and are able to form small islands further from shore, growing as they catch sediment to form nature's barrier to storm surges.

The black mangrove is tolerant of cooler weather and grows as far north as the Florida-Georgia border and was the primary victim of the die-off in Clam Bay that Kathy Worley cut her eyeteeth on.

Clam Bay

The Clam Bay estuary, to the west of Pelican Bay, consists of 600 acres of shallow sediment and sandy bottom bordered by mangroves and berms to manage storm water outflow. In the predevelopment era, it was fed from the Gulf of Mexico by three passes: Wiggins to the north, Doctor's to the south and Clam Pass in the center. Vanderbilt Beach Road, built in 1952, cut off the northern connection to the upper part of the bay and six years later Seagate Drive modified the connection between Doctor's Pass and the lower part of the bay. The one remaining direct tidal connection was the central pass which is dredged periodically to increase flow in and out of the bay. Clam Pass has no hardened structures so it moves as bordering sand and is driven by storms, Gulf currents, and some human intervention.

Deterioration of the mangrove forests began in 1984 but became obvious when the large die-off occurred in 1991. It continued and began to stretch south in 1995, probably due to inundation according to the most recent research "... altered soil chemistry, lack of tidal exchange, and high water surface and water retention contributed to the decline in productivity, growth and eventually death of the mangroves. The black mangroves were slowly dying for many years and rainfall events simply accelerated the process."[35]

Worley recalls the time when she first started working on the project. "There was simply no tidal flushing. But it wasn't just that, it was also the construction of roads and retention walls that restricted the groundwater flow through the estuary and contributed to longer retention times. I can also recall advocating for inquiry into the effect of storm sewer systems and still stand by those recommendations. Another answer is to channelize the bay but it's possible to overdo that, and it's only part of the solution."[36]

Exactly that was proposed in 2013 by constructing a bridge on Seagate Drive with a large conduit beneath to connect south Clam Bay to Venetian Bay and downstream to Doctors Pass. Engineering studies showed the project would further jeopardize the health of the mangroves and contribute to further instability of Clam Pass. The idea was summarily scotched.

After years of research, Worley is convinced that storm water runoff from urbanized areas into the black mangrove fringe during storm events occurs as pulse releases rather than predevelopment sheet flow that slowly percolates through the soil. Urban runoff carries with it a number of pollutants including herbicides and motor oil, both of which are highly toxic to mangroves. However, research shows that the biomass in mangrove forests is greatest where the trees can intercept terrestrial runoff nutrients such as phosphorus and nitrogen. The important element would be to strike a balance, and although Pelican Bay was designed to protect the mangroves, road building on the north and south perimeters of the estuary compromised the natural flow.

The second stressor is stagnation of the water rather than tidal movement. Worley concludes with this comment "... mangrove die-offs adjacent to development are lower in elevation and have higher water retention than mangroves located in areas that do not abut development. Under normal tidal conditions, oxygen concentrations decline in the pneumatophores during high tide and recover quickly during low tide. If extended periods of inundation occur, oxygen storage and exchange becomes compromised and oxygen in the system declines sharply thus, if pneumatophores are submerged for a prolonged period of time, black mangroves figuratively 'drown', and the result is mass mortality." [37]

Mangrove Research

With almost 40 years experience in Clam Bay, Worley feels that her research is driven by increasing frequency and intensity of weather events due to global warming leading to different stressors manifest in the mangrove forests. The trees are able to withstand storm surge but not wind and combining the two in coastal forests produces a devastating outcome as do heavy inland rains washing urban runoff out into the estuaries.

The Intergovernmental Panel on Climate Change (IPCC) recognizes the protective value of mangroves and the need to promote their role in building shorelines as sediment accumulates around the roots but the problem, Worley admits, is that science moves slowly. It is based upon uncertainty, upon testing hypotheses with vast amounts of data, and subjecting conclusions to peer review.

Current science is still in flux. "At this point, any discussion of the effect of accelerated sea level rise on mangrove ecosystems in Florida remains speculative. It is likely that mangroves can keep pace with relatively high rates of sea level rise if sedimentation rates are high. Since sedimentation rates are highly territorial in different locations in Florida, some areas will probably keep pace with sea level rise and some will become inundated. In the latter case, if the shore gradient is low—as occurs along the lower Southwest coast of Florida—mangrove swamps will simply roll over in an inland direction. The result will be steady or even increased mangrove area." [38]

Another recent study concludes "... initial modeling attempt suggests that moderate rates of sea level rise along the lower southwest coast of Florida would result in an increase in mangrove area." [39]

Mangroves would form an important part of a future collaboration between science and policy when Collier County brings in the U.S. Army Corps of Engineers to look at ways to prevent coastal flooding from storm surge during hurricanes. It would bring Worley back into the discussion and put the Conservancy at the forefront of nature-based solutions.

To that point, Worley is very specific. "The relationship between science and policy at the Conservancy has always been a moving target. Early on, Bernie Yokel's work and Dave Addison's sea turtle research informed policy. When Jim Gore was here, he tended more toward policy than science. David Guggenheim firewalled the two. So did Benedict to a certain degree. But my feeling is when we do work in areas like water quality, it leads to policy choices that are important for our region. We don't have to be fully firewalled because we are stronger together."[40]

Pythons

The lab is clean and populated only by piles of eggs larger than those we find in the supermarket and a few coiled serpents parked on shelves around the edge of the room. The only exception is a large tub in which lies a coiled snake submerged in fluid. *Python bivittatus* is the scientific name but to residents of southwest Florida she is more commonly known as the Burmese python.

"That's tomorrow's project," says Ian Bartozek. "We're going to cut her open and see how many eggs she carries. We caught her a few days ago and she looks like she may be five years old. At that age she is in her prime reproductive period."

Bartozek is sitting in front of a large screen prepared to manipulate a series of maps showing the locations over time of the pythons found in southwest Florida. He is earnest and forthcoming about his lifelong love of snakes.

"When I was a kid in Miami, I had a couple of albino pythons in my room. In the '90s they were very common and they were great escape artists. They would get loose in the house and it would take me hours to find them. Some of my friends had them too, but their fascination was as much with feeding mice while mine was with studying the nature and adaptations of their pets. I didn't like the idea of feeding mice and what really fascinated me was how something with no arms and legs was able to move around. Of course I had other animals as pets but I think the pythons were my favorites."

Bartozek then went on to the University of Arizona, graduating with a degree in wildlife and fisheries science. He came directly to the Conservancy and began doing biological monitoring of the Picayune Strand Restoration Project.

Origins

How the Burmese python, an apex predator, first appeared, began to thrive, and eventually eat its way through the Everglades from the east to the west coast of Florida is a complicated story.

One of the largest snakes in the world, it originated in southeast Asia. There are records of Burmese pythons in the United States as early as 1900 and one report noted a python in the Everglades in 1912. Another was collected as roadkill in 1979. There were some sightings in Everglades National Park in the 1980s, but only as undocumented observations. It became popular in the United States in the 1990s when more than 90,000 snakes were imported into the country as pets.

One theory of how the Florida population became large enough to be reproductively viable occurred after hurricane

Andrew in 1992 when python breeding facilities and zoos were damaged allowing the animals to escape and spread into the central Everglades. This theory may apply to part of the population because there is considerable evidence that the species in the western section of South Florida is slightly separate from those in the central Everglades.

However, reproductive viability depends on a scenario where a relatively large number of snakes would have to be released, so the theory is that there was a release of a number of either juvenile or adult pet pythons in Everglades National Park or near Flamingo probably prior to 1985. That cluster then moved north toward Lake Okeechobee through the park and the water management areas south of the Everglades Agricultural Area. Observations began to occur because the population had grown to a level through multiple generations to the point where it had spread and achieved an observable level of density.

A second cluster probably originated in the mid to late 1990s according to Bartozek, before the central Everglades population spread further west. According to a number of studies, by the year 2000 sightings were common and documented throughout the Fakahatchee, along SR 29, throughout the Big Cypress National Preserve and in other natural areas east and north of I-75.

In southwest Florida, hatchlings were observed just outside the City of Naples in 2011. The first egg laying python was observed in 2012 near the Loop Road of US 41.

To the south they have been found as far as Key Largo and to the east along the outskirts of the City of Miami and north to the Caloosahatchee River in Lee County. The fairly rapid spread is probably due to the extensive network of canals and water management systems south of the Caloosahatchee and St. Lucie Rivers. Pythons are excellent swimmers and the immediate availability of canals might have become a highway network facilitating the diaspora. Bartozek is not sure of this because of possible predation by alligators and other predators—particularly of juveniles.

The survival rate of juvenile pythons is approximately 5%. Females are able to lay more eggs as they grow older, so the numbers vary depending upon the age of the snake. By averaging research, the average is approximately 40 eggs per laying season. Assuming this is correct it would mean that two juveniles survive to adulthood. Given the current rate of removal it's obvious why the population is growing.

Morphology

Females tend to be slightly longer than the males and much heavier and larger. The longest one ever captured in southwest Florida measured a little over 17 feet and the longest ever caught in the world was at 18'10". It weighed over 400 pounds.

Pythons are secretive by nature, able to conceal themselves in vegetation which, because of their coloration, makes them nearly invisible from a distance. In southwest

Florida those captured by Bartozek had a "... irregular, maze-like dorsal pattern consistent with a 'labyrinth' morph."

Their preferred habitats are marshes, swamps and some upland areas that perfectly describes much of the public lands in southwest Florida. They have been found in virtually all habitats but prefer animal holes like gopher tortoise burrows during the day because they are nocturnal hunters. The python can both climb and swim. It needs a permanent source of water nearby and can stay submerged for 30 minutes or more. After a recent hurricane, one snake was found 15 miles offshore swimming in the Gulf of Mexico

They are carnivores. They have relatively long fasting periods, generally feeding once every two or three weeks. Diet tends to consist of birds and mammals but can include amphibians and reptiles. They are ambush predators using cues to "identify trails left by prey species and then conceal themselves near grade pathways striking when prey approaches." [41] They use their infrared sensitive scales and heat-sensing openings on upper lips to detect warm-blooded prey as it approaches. As they grow they graduate to larger prey being able to unhinge their jaws to swallow large mammals. There have been some examples photographed by Conservancy scientists of both alligators and adult deer eaten by pythons.

The Conservancy's Bartozek has been conducting necropsy of diets for seven years. He found that small rodents such as cotton and black rats comprise a great deal of the diet along with mice and marsh rabbits as well as muskrats. A total of 48 species of birds have been identified as well as larger mammals with a total taxa of 76 different species.

Pythons use short rearward-facing teeth to seize prey. They then curl their bodies around the animal and with each exhale squeeze a little tighter until the prey suffocates.

After they kill the digestive system changes by increasing stomach acid. The ventricle in the lower part of the heart increases in mass and is accompanied by a dramatic increase in oxygen consumption. The system then produces hydrochloric acid allowing the snake to break down the animal without the use of teeth, eventually reducing it to a semi-liquid form that can be passed into the lower intestine.

Pythons and their prey share one aversion—and that is to populated and urbanized areas. As a consequence, the Everglades ecosystem is almost perfectly adapted to their expansion. There is no mortally cold weather in South Florida and the python is able to cope easily with the flooding rains of summer and an occasional hurricane, with the only natural predators being alligators finding and eating pythons in their juvenile state and humans hunting them.

Into the U.S.

Many snakes are bred for a unique color or pattern. A hybrid of the Burmese python was introduced to the commercial pet trade in 1989.[42] One particular labyrinth morph[43] does not appear in the southeast Florida population and the difference in coloration indicates that the southwest population is somewhat differentiated from that on the east coast, meaning the origins of the two were separate.

This theory has been heavily debated. The first recorded sighting in southwest Florida occurred in 2003 and another in 2005 near Everglades City. At the time, most of the sightings had been recorded further to the east. Given that the population density needs to reach a certain level for the animals to be observed, Bartozek thinks they may have been introduced in the mid to late 1990s.

CISMA

In 2012, Bartozek was deputized as lead of the Southwest Florida Cooperative Invasive Species Management Area (CISMA) a group run by the Florida Fish and Wildlife Conservation Commission. He had been on a number of other scientific projects for the Conservancy but was recruited by Greg Curry at Rookery Bay National Estuarine Research Reserve where they were working on establishing a system using telemetry transmitters. He was in seventh heaven; he was now the primary researcher and he was back in the field. It also offered him an opportunity to create baseline data on a large scale. "This is a novel situation. I am studying one of the largest predators on the planet as it eats its way through one of the world's most unique ecosystems." Given that the study area covered 100 sq. mi., he would eventually capture over 15 tons of snakes in the next 10 years.

Rookery Bay, a hot bed of local python activity, deployed a removal program beginning in 2015. The State of Florida, through the efforts of the Fish and Wildlife Conservation Commission and the south Florida Water Management District, began to implement removal programs in South Florida in 2017. Up until that time most of the telemetry work had been done to create scientific baseline data but as the python population grew it created an imbalance in the ecosystem with a number of species of small mammals and birds being severely impacted by predation. The idea was to mitigate the effect on native fauna to preserve the biodiversity of the Everglades ecosystem.

The reverse effect has been noted in some research studies. When evaluating the nesting success of egg laying species, particularly sea turtles along the coast, data has shown that predation rates were higher where there were few or no pythons present and measurably lower where the snakes were within the vicinity. The studies concluded that there was a direct suppression of predators such as raccoons and feral hogs.[44]

Removal

The Conservancy uses something called the Judas technique for removal. Breeding age males are captured during the mating season and a subcutaneous transmitter, with a life of 2 to 3 years, is embedded. The scout snakes are then released back into the wild to roam and reveal the females' location. According to Bartozek each scout can locate an average of five females—then they are brought in and euthanized.

Using telemetry data, Conservancy research indicates that the males cover about 2.6 sq. mi. while a typical female will only cover 1.09 sq. mi. of territory—typical mating and nesting activity.

The scout program is more expensive than cruising roads for visual identification and it's able to detect large snakes that may not be otherwise seen. Telemetry has been assisted by drones but requires active human capture in a hostile environment, and Bartozek admits that he has a limited future. "I tend to have a five-year horizon. That's probably a pretty good blueprint for the county and the region. I love this job because it puts the Conservancy on the map and in the field, but it's hard work and requires slogging through some rough terrain. But our study over the past 10 years has created large scale baseline data. It's important, and our work is going to make a significant difference in the management of this invasive species."

The scout snake program is only one of a number of removal programs.

A second method used for a number of invasive and destructive species is trapping. Using funnel or reptile traps covered by game cameras is effective where there is little immediate access. While useful, the technique has not been widely successful because detection tends to rely upon the heat signatures of prey moving about and not lying stationary inside a trap.

Another less well-known technique uses pheromones, chemical compounds that communicate breeding readiness, but there is little or no research involving the Burmese python.

Finally there are the python hunts. One of the earliest was the Python Challenge in 2013. Prizes were offered for the biggest, longest and greatest numbers of snakes captured, and after one month 68 had been removed. It gave politicians a series of unforgettable photo ops and did increase awareness of the problem, but did little to dent the rapidly growing population.

When Bartozek began his work in Rookery Bay in 2012 there was one capture. Ten years later, 383 Burmese pythons were captured in southwest Florida. The current population is estimated at over 10,000.

Future

Carrying the conversation into the future, Bartozek opined: "I think that one area that has not been adequately studied is the use of CRISPR technology and genetic control. That might offer some help as it has worked with other species, but it's expensive."

When asked about the future of the southwest Florida ecosystem, Bartozek was reflective: "The python is really shuffling the deck in the Everglades. I think nature has a way of evolving and coping with different threats and eventually will strike a balance with the python. My work is interesting because it involves an invasive species. The

Conservancy science department also has a long-term study about the sea turtles—an endangered species—over 40 years of data there. We are all working for the same goal whether invasive or endangered and my hope is that the politics will follow the science. And while we are making a lot of progress, my last piece of advice is: don't ever underestimate the Burmese python."

Rob Moher also has very strong opinions about the future of the Conservancy's python project. "Right now we are the center of world attention. We are a center of excellence in python research, the only nonprofit involved and we have an opportunity to attract partners because the story is so compelling and the destruction of the Everglades is so significant. We have the infrastructure and the talent and reputation to attract partners like large companies that want to be involved in the solution."

Policy

The next set of chapters covers growth management in eastern Collier and Lee counties, a takeover by the State of Florida of permitting for destruction of native and natural wetlands and a proposal by the Corps of Engineers to harden the coastline of Collier County.

While growth management occupied a great deal of time and attention by the Conservancy during the last decade, that concern was shared by the residents of Collier County. The 2022–2023 Collier County Community Assessment funded by the Richard Schulze Family Foundation found that in the five-year period from 2017–2018 that managing growth and development as a community priority had risen dramatically from 38% to 63%, a close second in priorities to controlling housing costs particularly for workforce housing at 65%. The environment, meaning planning, preservation and emergency coastal resilience and storm mitigation, ended up in third place at 41%. Only 7% of the respondents were satisfied with climate change readiness by the county, and 42% were not. Based upon those three leading priorities and findings, the work of the Conservancy takes on even greater importance.[45]

Following that, the focus turns to Lee County, where protective zoning overlays, in place for decades, were being either cancelled or ignored and where rampant development affected one of southwest Florida's greatest natural assets—Audubon's Corkscrew Swamp Sanctuary. It's a tough and ongoing story.

There is a very important point here, one recognized by the Conservancy's policy team, and that is that while Lee and Collier counties are two entirely separate geopolitical subdivisions they were once a single and unified entity when it came to watershed and flow ways. Historically there was no separation, but now with roads and canals, and despite recent attempts to restore natural conditions, there is little left without engineered interruptions as shown on the Page 61 map.

Rob Moher has very specific thoughts about framing the issue of growth management. "I think we make a mistake by always referring to the 'eastern lands.' It is much more than that; it is in fact the western Everglades, a unified ecosystem. The problems are being created by new people coming into southwest Florida who have little appreciation for the importance and beauty of the wilderness. We have uncontrolled growth enabled by pliant legislators with a blatant disregard for existing growth management plans and zoning codes. And finally there is the greed—the desire to get in and get out and make as much money as quickly as possible. Taken together it is a dangerous combination."

We will then examine in detail the frenzied rush by the State of Florida to take over all permitting for the destruction of nature's kidney—native wetlands—in the few weeks before the Trump administration left office. It turned out to be a sloppy and unfinished transition, causing the Conservancy and its partners to take the offending parties to court.

Next comes a chapter on a recent proposal by the U.S. Army Corps of Engineers to reduce the effects of storm surge during hurricanes. It too was hurried, and the Conservancy took a lead position in slowing the process.

In the struggle to save the natural world of southwest Florida, replete with its precious resources and indigenous species, nothing is sacred except the siren song of money to be made, and there are no wars to be won but always just another battle to be fought until the land is finally placed into public ownership. And even then it may be in jeopardy. And in its policy initiatives the Conservancy is critical to further exposing the fissures in overdevelopment and in offering solutions through the education of both citizens and public officials.

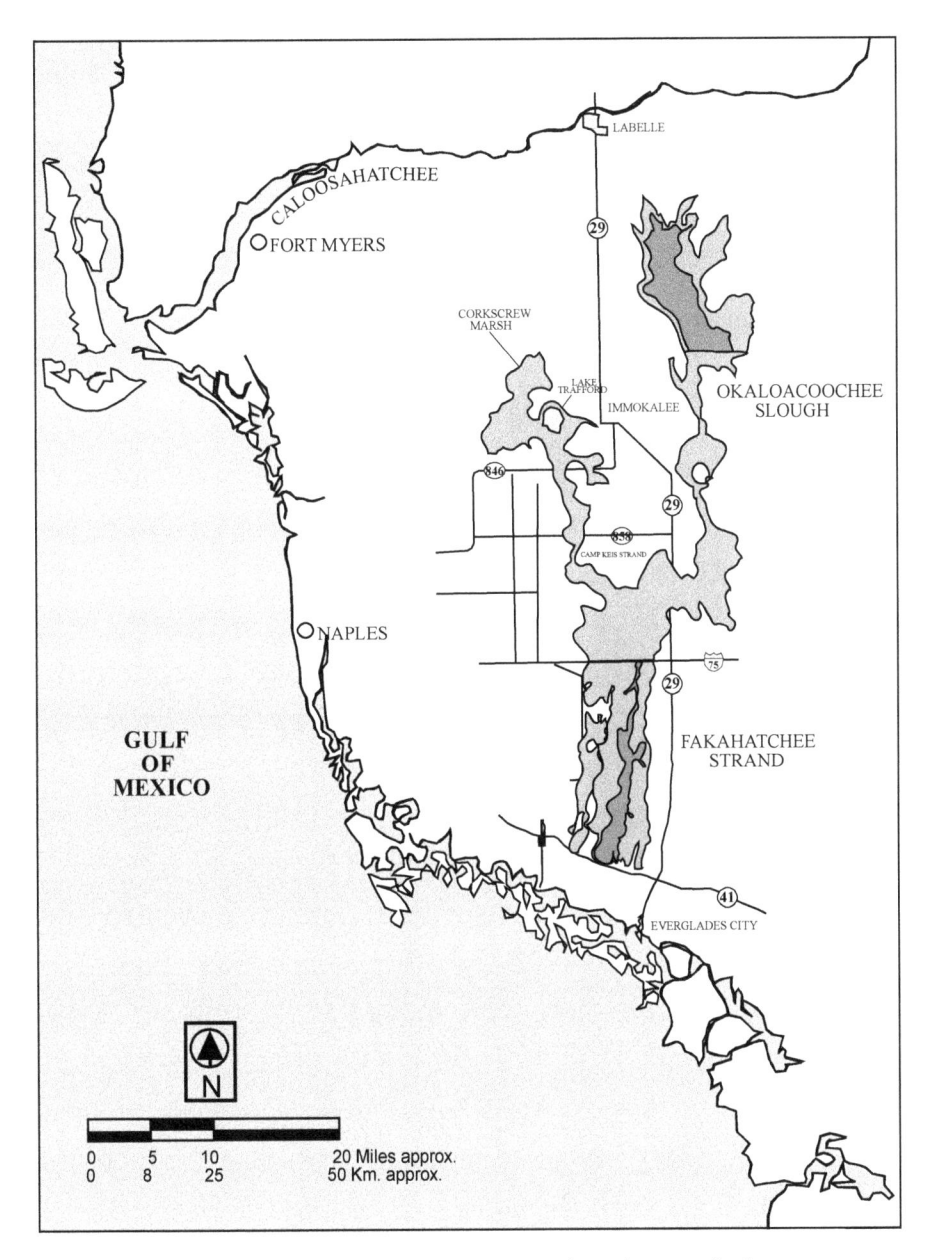

Major flow ways from Lee County map by: John G. Beriault

Rural Lands Stewardship Area

In 1945 the population of Florida was about 2.5 million. By 2020 it had reached 10 million and was the fastest growing state in the country.[46] The state legislature and governor's office had been in the hands of yellow dog Democrats since Reconstruction, but in 1967 a Republican, Claude Kirk, took office. He was followed by two Democrats, Ruben Askew and Bob Graham, then another Republican Bill Martinez, Democrat Lawton Chiles and finally, from 1998 to 2007 Republican Jeb Bush.

The state legislature was moving steadily toward one party domination. By 1992 the State Senate was tied at 20-20 and the next election cycle moved to Republican 21-19. The House was 63-57 in 1994 with a Democrat majority but then flipped in 1996 to 61-59 Republican. Once established the majority party began to redistrict resulting in tectonic changes by 2022 with the Senate 28-12 and the House 85-35.

With an earlier history of bipartisan cooperation in a generally progressive legislature, the State of Florida passed a series of overall growth management plans beginning in 1972 and broadly codified in 1985. It created regional planning councils (RPCs) for large development projects affecting multiple counties and oversaw coordination between the state's plan and comprehensive plans from each county. The process was designed to be iterative, moving from local county commissions up to Tallahassee at the Department of Community Affairs (DCA) and back down again. DCA's job was to provide "...regulatory oversight of planning, review developments with regional impact, and provide technical assistance to local governments developing strategies for growth."[47] Local plans were mandated but by 1979 a number of local governments had not created comprehensive plans.

Under Gov. Bob Graham, in office from 1979 to 1987, a number of major changes took place particularly in the Omnibus Growth Management Plan of 1985 incorporating a number of coastal construction laws which would have a dramatic effect on Collier County. At the time, the state's policy was to encourage development with a range of public amenities as well as affordable housing. In 1987, the state had clearly established the need for "concurrency" where local governments would assess and collect impact fees to cover the cost of public services including schools and roads. By 1992, comprehensive plans had been submitted to the state by 455 of the 458 local governments. Collier County was among them, but its plan was heavily criticized and subject to constant renegotiation so was never fully implemented.

In 1999, DCA was losing patience. Collier County was warned that its rather sketchy growth management plan did not coordinate with that of the state. Finally, after more futile back and forth, DCA filed an administrative complaint, threatening a lawsuit to back it up, asserting its regulatory authority and forcing the county to confront the situation.

The Board of County Commissioners (BCC), to avoid litigation, created an advisory committee known as the Rural Lands Assessment Oversight Committee (RLAOC). It was composed of a broad range of interested and affected parties with a citrus grower, Ron Hamel, appointed as chair and an environmental advocate, Charles Lee, as Vice-Chair.

The study process took over 2½ years with a number of public meetings and was presented to the commission in April 2002. It covered 182,000 acres of privately owned land of the 195,000 acres in the Rural Lands Stewardship Area (RLSA).

The result was well thought out and unanimously supported by the committee. It sought to encourage compact clustered development (as opposed to sprawl) through incentives, to preserve wildlife habitat and corridors, to move development away from water recharge and retention areas and flow ways, and to protect and encourage agriculture as an alternative to further development consistent with the expressed intent of the program. The underlying zoning in the county—base density—was one home per five acres at the time and by increasing density through incentives, it was expected that compact development would become the hallmark of the rural lands.

The committee's assumptions about growth had been based on the Metropolitan Planning Organization's (MPO) 2025 population projections. The estimated number of homes with underlying density would amount to a little over 36,000, and by increasing density to a little over two units per acre 16,800 acres would be needed for rural development.

This calculation was based a upon a complex system of credits in which individual parcels were given multiple land use layers beginning with residential, then moving down through conditional uses, mining, recreation, and finally three levels of agriculture.

As a first step, each parcel would be evaluated for environmental elements, beginning with (a) flow ways and water retention areas, (b) proximity to stewardship areas, (c) listed species habitat, (d) soils and surface water indices, (e) restoration potential and (f) land use based on the FLUCCS code, a habitat-based approach to assess the needs and status of wildlife in Florida.[48] The highest premium value was placed on known primary panther habitat and on flow ways, namely the Camp Keais and Okaloacoochee Sloughs. Each had an assigned value based upon relative importance to create a Natural Resource Index (NRI) for each parcel using a geographic imaging system (GIS) and modeling.

Land with high resource values would be designated as Stewardship Sending Areas (SSA) and the credit system

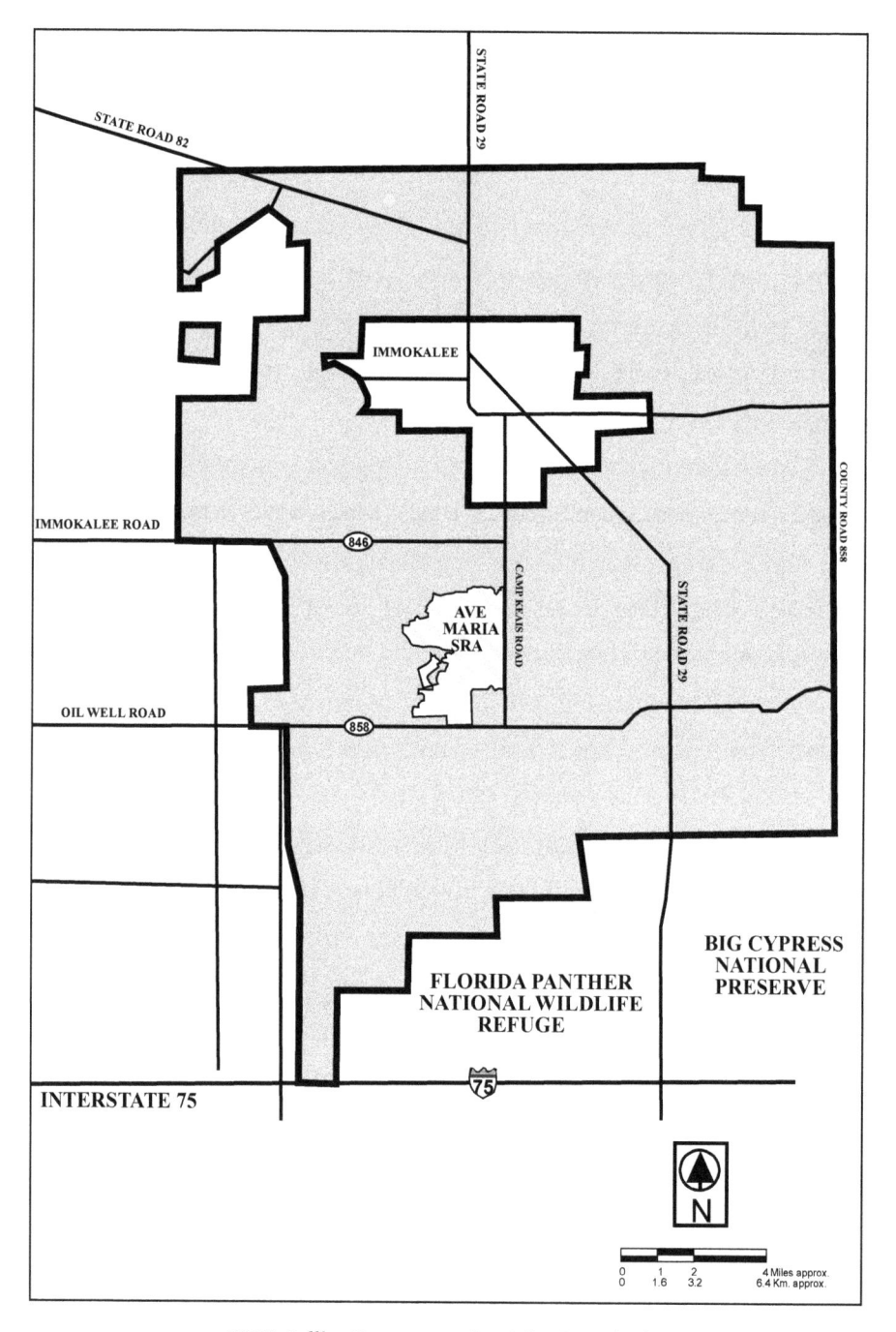

RLSA Collier County map by: John G. Beriault

would give owners of important natural areas an economic incentive to place property in conservation easements in perpetuity.

Development would occur in Stewardship Receiving Areas (SRAs). Both designations would be effective upon petition by a property owner and development would have to be in accordance with the growth management plan and land development code. A third category, Neutral Areas (NA), would remain undesignated when the program began and subject to later review. Finally, along the borders of developed areas buffers would be required in the transition to adjacent lands of significantly lower density.

An SSA land owner above a certain threshold could then strip off use layers and by multiplying those times the number of acres, obtain stewardship credits which could be sold to developers for increased density and other items requiring bonus credits.[49] As a further incentive, multiplier values were available based upon certain criteria such as the substantiated presence of endangered species—bringing about a higher multiplier making the property's value increase.[50]

In cases where developers owned land designated as SSA, they could simply pledge credits to projects being built in the SRAs, which would work well for Barron Collier Companies and Collier Enterprises, both owning substantial acreage and both participating in the program. Since most of the land in eastern Collier County was owned by a few large operations they could generally use their own land as offsets. The credit market was really intended for smaller landowners.

The effort was supported in Tallahassee. At the state level, the Florida Rural Lands Stewardship Act, passed in 2001 as a pilot program and fully codified in 2004, was designed to provide landowners with economic incentives to protect environmental areas, wildlife habitat and agriculture. The language stated "... It is the intent of the legislature that land stewardship areas be used to further the following broad principles of rural sustainability: restoration and maintenance of the economic value; control of urban sprawl; identification and protection of ecosystems habitats, and natural resources; promotion of rural economic activity; maintenance of the viability of Florida agriculture; and protection of the character of rural areas of Florida."[51] A stewardship area had to be initiated at the behest of landowners with a 10,000-acre minimum. Once a plan was adopted, local government was required to pass an ordinance creating a zoning overlay.

The intent was laudable. It sought to move from a regulatory to an incentive-based approach. It attempted to modify the traditional antagonism between environmental advocates and property owners by using a system of transferable credits to protect important natural resources.

What was not obvious in the initial calculation process for the Collier program, based upon eight SSA credits per acre, was a recommendation of additional credits for restoration on a case-by-case basis. The RLAOC report did not quantify the impact of these credits on the original 16,508 acres and it was never overtly considered in transmittal documents, but DCA in Tallahassee asked that county staff quantify the additional credits.

No longer to be called out on a case-by-case basis, restoration and early entry bonus credits were added, with additional credits for restoration and completion by permitting agencies. As a result of private meetings between the landowners and some environmental organizations, credits increased from the Transmittal document to the Adoption version to 315,000, increasing the development footprint to 39,375 acres. The public was not aware of this until later.

In December 2002, DCA approved the county's GMP amendments incorporating recommendations of the study committee, but one thing was missing. There was no limitation to the development footprint at build out.

Blessed by the State

The adopted plan was subject to review in five years. A Five-year Review Committee (FRC) was formed in 2007 but the membership was tilted more heavily toward development interests than in 2000. The story of the Conservancy's involvement in the process was extensively covered in *Nature's Steward: A History of the Conservancy of Southwest Florida,* published by Pineapple Press in 2014, so will not be duplicated in detail here.

In summary, the revisions marked a departure from the 2002 adopted plan. FRC recommendations presented in 2008 were acceptable to the County Commission but never adopted for two reasons. The landowners applying for the overlay refused to pay for a special amendment to the GMP and the real estate market in Florida was beginning to collapse.

By 2009, with the real estate industry in deep doldrums, the Republican legislature passed a single sweeping change to the state's growth management oversight by exempting the transportation concurrency element from impact fees.

Concurrency had been the most significant piece of the Gov. Graham's 1985 Omnibus Act. It shifted the cost of infrastructure like water, sewer and roads from the taxpayer to the developer. In the late 1990s, as the legislature was moving toward the political right, schools became a major issue with both sides of the aisle in Tallahassee, with both Gov. Chiles and Gov. Bush concerned about the quality of education. After much debate, building schools became part of concurrency. The DRI program came under assault and while the underlying sentiment was to leave it out it was modified. Certain elements were exempted, but the growth management system put in place in 1985 remained largely intact, until 2011.

Ave Maria

Taking advantage of the new program, the Barron Collier Companies formed a partnership with Tom Monaghan, founder of Domino's Pizza. Ave Maria SRA was approved by the Florida legislature in 2004. A limited local government entity, called a stewardship district, was formed in 2005 to provide infrastructure in the community to include a university.[52] The town was initially 5,027 acres, 4,000 acres of commercial and residential development in the 1,027 acres for the university. The school was deemed to be a public benefit, so the acreage was exempted from the required transfer of credits.

The build out plan was for 11,000 homes with about 25,000 residents. The university anticipated a student population of 5,000. The project was a good illustration of how the program might work. 28,658 credits were used, taken from 13,974 acres of SSA's, so the ratio of developed land to preserved was about 2½ times (net of the public benefit land).

The timing was terrible. Florida was rocked by a housing recession in 2008–2009 just as Ave Maria was starting to sell homes.[53] The town bumped through a few problems with water supply but sales began to accelerate during the 2019 and 2020 COVID crisis and went into overdrive in 2021. By 2023 approximately 4,000 homes had been built.

To accommodate anticipated growth, the County Commission authorized the addition of 1,000 acres to bring the town to 5,000 acres—the maximum allowed. The annexed land had been used for crops, sod farming and cows. A new (third) town center would be built with homes by large national companies like Lennar and Del Webb, emphasizing a listing price significantly lower than either Miami or Naples. Part of the motivation was that over half of the new buyers in 2023 were coming from Miami-Dade and Broward Counties on the east coast.

In a way this was a harbinger of what would become a parade of new subdivisions being pushed aggressively through the permitting process. Ave Maria was 26 miles east of Naples and could become a bedroom community for people working in the western parts of Broward and Miami-Dade counties via US 29 and I-75. This fact was not lost on Collier Enterprises.

Opening the Eastern Lands of the Western Everglades

In 2006, Collier Enterprises had unveiled plans to build 25,000 homes in the Town of Big Cypress with a scattering of smaller villages on 8,000 acres of farmland surrounded by some 14,000 acres of preserve stretching from Immokalee Road to I-75 and end east of Golden Gate Estates. The initial build-out would be a big-box shopping center.

The company justified the planned construction sequence based on a lack of available retail space near the Estates. Tom Flood, CEO of Collier Enterprises said the town would ultimately include 830,000 square feet for commercial space, over 800,000 square feet of offices and 500,000 square feet for light industrial, a golf course, a 500-room hotel, a 200-bed hospital, civic buildings and multiple parks.

Tim Nance, president of the Golden Gate Estates Area Civic Association, was supportive: "People are looking forward to some commercial development out there," he said. "It's nice when you can use roads both ways, instead of one direction in the morning and the other coming home at night."

Nance also backed a proposed I-75 interchange from Everglades Boulevard east to Collier Enterprises-owned lands. Flood said the company was working with the county to determine the feasibility of moving the interchange supported by Connie Deane, spokeswoman for Collier County's transportation division, who said the county expected approval within one year.

But the company quickly changed its mind and announced plans a little over a year later for a smaller development to be known as Rural Lands West that would include 10,000 residential units on 4,000 acres in eastern Collier County. The downsized plan, submitted to the local RPC, envisaged a town center encircled by a realignment of Oil Well Road and an extension of Randall Boulevard. Taken out were proposals for villages and hamlets farther north and south on existing Collier holdings. That would come later. The company anticipated starting in late 2010, with the first phase completed by 2020, finishing build out by 2023.

Flood, while not openly admitting it, sensed that the real estate market in southwest Florida was changing. And he was right for in 2008 it began to tank and in February 2010 he decided to delay permitting. Part of the idea behind the delay was to file with the USFWS for a 45,000-acre Habitat Conservation Plan (HCP) in conjunction with a group of local and state conservation organizations including Florida Wildlife Federation, Defenders of Wildlife, Audubon of Florida, and Collier County Audubon Society (now Audubon of the Western Everglades). The Conservancy had been asked to join but declined based upon the proposition that membership required total allegiance and buy-in to an uncertain future.

Conservancy President, Andrew McElwaine, explained that he had the organization's science staff analyze the environmental effects of the new plan and while he approved the idea of building the town center between Oil Well Road and Randall Boulevard, he had concerns about the effect on wetlands and panther habitat. And in fact, he was also bothered by the possibility, although not in the proposal at the time, that habitat in the southern portion of the larger (initial) stewardship district, very close to the Florida Panther National Wildlife Refuge, would be impacted if the project expanded. It would come back later, as a subdivision called Bellmar.

Within the boundaries of the initial proposal, 850 acres were wetlands to be preserved. Development would occur mostly on cleared farmland. The project would destroy 180 acres of wetlands, according to company figures, but as an offset, the company planned to set aside 7,000 acres running 10-miles along a strip of the western edge of the

Camp Keais Strand south from Lake Trafford. The company promised to preserve another 3,000 acres of wetlands in the Okaloacoochee Slough east of Immokalee.

The process for high level review of large projects was soon doomed. Rick Scott had moved to Florida in 2003, retiring from his job as CEO of Columbia/HCA Hospital Company. In 2000, his company agreed to pay more than $840 million in fines and damages for unlawful billing practices, and an additional $881 million fine was levied bringing the total to $1.7 billion.[54] Scott then ran for governor in 2010, funded mostly by his own wealth to the tune of over $60 million, and won.[55] In 2011, he folded DCA into something called the Department of Economic Development, effectively eliminating the state's comprehensive plan and, as part of the process, neutered the Regional Planning Councils.

A New Look at Growth Management— The Restudy

Tim Nance was elected County Commissioner from District 5 in 2016, which included Golden Gate Estates and Immokalee. He served one term and was a thoughtful and engaged member of the county board. Aware of the difficulties and differences in attempting to reconcile the first RLSA project with FRC's work in 2008 and 2009, he proposed that the county bring in a set of outside eyes to look at how development should occur within his district.

To do that the county promoted Kris Van Lengen as Community Planning Manager. A lawyer by training with a master's degree in public administration, he had been the county's growth management department, then in Marco Island for two years as city planner and had returned to the county as the utility department's environmental compliance manager before being asked to head the restudy. Most important, he was an experienced executive with no preconceptions or entwinement with the special interests abundant in Collier County at the time.

He would be assisted by Anita Jenkins, a former employee of Wilson Miller (now Stantec), the company that had done the first RLSA overlay and credit system. She understood how the natural resource index credits were created and how the system should work, so was an ideal partner for Van Lengen.

For purposes of public input and transparency, the County Commission created an *ad hoc* committee called the Growth Management Oversight Committee (GMOC) to act in an advisory capacity and create a series of public meetings to be held in each of the four areas to be restudied, those being Immokalee, Golden Gate Estates, the Rural Fringe Mixed Use District (RFMUD)[56] and 195,000-acre eastern lands. The committee was composed of residents of each of the restudy areas with three at-large members.[57] It was engaged and heard presentations on storm water management, affordable housing, transportation, listed and endangered species, and other topics pertinent to land-use planning.

The final product after public meetings on each of the restudy areas was a series of white papers presented to the Collier County Planning Commission (CCPC) and ultimately County Commission for their consideration and incorporation into the GMP. The Golden Gate Estates plan was well received, as were the RFMUD suggestions. The Immokalee restudy had the advantage of another group's prior analysis so was somewhat familiar to the commissioners. The Chamber of Commerce worked for years to amend the Area Master Plan and it was updated with some improvements.

The rural lands were a different matter. As brought forward before, the FRC had attempted to quantify the number of credits, both baseline and bonus, in the 2002 adopted plan. It then added new credits for agricultural protection and improvement of wildlife corridors as part of a larger panther protection program much favored by some of the environmental partners.

Since restoration credits were primarily responsible for the startling increase in the development footprint, adding some 160,000 credits or 20,000 new acres, a small attempt was made to reduce the footprint by increasing credits required for SRAs from 8 to 10 per acre.

A series of six public meetings were held during 2018, one for each of the policy groups: (1) general purposes; (2) agricultural protection; (3) environmental protection; (4) responsible development; (5) lands not included in the program; and finally, an evaluation and attempt to reconcile differences of opinions.

In the meetings confusion reigned over the two different restoration credits. R-1 was for the "dedication" of land with no changes. Once the land was designated as R-1 any public agency could come in and do restoration. R-2 was for "completion" of activities by the owner or owner's agent that modified and/or rehabilitated existing land within the HSAs, FSAs and any other acreage within 500' of protected areas—all to preserve functionality. The justification was that the cost of mitigation would run between $4,000 and $5,000 per acre. On the other hand, Conservation Collier had been buying sensitive land for up to $20,000 per acre. By giving private owners credits to do the work made economic sense and would remove it from taxpayers having to pay the freight.

While the economic argument was sound, Nicole Johnson of the Conservancy pointed out in one meeting that some credits, the R-1 credits, could be made available for doing nothing, and needed to be further refined in the new program. A second problem was the fact that credits could be given for isolated parcels without some consideration of the creation and value of wildlife corridors and large swaths of adjacent habitat. A suggestion was made to update mapping in the SSAs with Critical Lands and Waters Identification Project (CLIP) data, and integrating the restoration credit system into other opportunities like Conservation Collier and Florida Forever to create large contiguous spaces and corridors for wildlife.

The biggest stated concern during the public meetings was that "...the credit system is inordinately complex and may be complex intentionally to be manipulated to benefit the group using it. It's so complex, it seems like funny money they generated to achieve predetermined goals." [58] The lack of accountability for completing the R-2 work according to established criteria was an issue since the land would be lost for agriculture—which was the original reason for creating the RLSA

The second area of concern was the NRI index. It had been created by Wilson Miller from open-source data, but the original had somehow disappeared from the company's files. While this created suspicion among audience members Alan Reynolds, responsible for creating the initial indices, insisted that the data had been turned over to the County, and could be re-created through an Internet search.

April Olson of the Conservancy was convinced that not all of the data had been turned over. According to the minutes of the January 31, 2019, meeting: "[she] said that there is information that Mr. Reynolds is not sharing. She said that every acre of land was given a score in 2002. She said based on the score given in 2002 anything over 1.3 is considered environmentally sensitive and under 1.3 is considered not environmentally sensitive. She said the data from 2002 should be shared with the public because it is the starting point. She would like to know where the original scores came from." [59]

After all was said and done, there was no clear consensus among participants, and the planning team regrouped to put its thoughts together and to produce an 89-page white paper appended with minutes from the public meetings.

Enter Thaddeus Cohen

In July 2017, Thaddeus Cohen was hired to head the Growth Management Department, to oversee construction and planning in the county. He would be responsible for implementing the revised GMP being worked on by Van Lengen and his small staff.

Cohen had headed DCA from 2004 to 2007 under Gov. Jeb Bush, the same department shut down by Gov. Scott. After leaving, he worked as the assistant city manager of Pensacola. "In 2015, he was hired as the planning director of Key West. He served there until March, when he was asked to resign by the Key West city manager, according to local news reports."[60]

Cohen was a large man. He had his own architectural firm before going into government work and was well-schooled in the art of political double-speak.

At the October 2019 commission meeting he made a polished presentation of staff recommendations, opening with the following statement: "We wanted to bring forward the Growth Management Plan amendments for the rural lands' stewardship area overlay as presented by the Five-year Review Committee and presented in the RLSA white paper. It's a process that you are very much familiar with.

We did the same thing for the Golden Gate as well as Immokalee area master plans in which we've had public workshops. We did an analysis, generated white paper, and will request from you the ability to repair amendments to move forward. What's the basis of us being able to move forward? We think, first of all, we've been in limbo for almost over a decade only due to lack of agreement as to who is going to pay for these amendments. The Five-year Review Committee recommendations have been prepared in underline and strikethrough."[61]

With that, it was "game over" for the restudy.

Cohen's plan was to create a single track for the FRC plan and a separate track for the white paper. During his presentation, he deftly conflated the two, but the white paper contained 51 recommendations and the "combined" staff document only 18 of those. Cohen also knew the likelihood, once his recommendations were put into a transmittal document and approved, that the white paper would eventually gather dust and be little more than a footnote to history.

Kris Van Lengen had abruptly left the county in August 2019 ostensibly to spend more time with his family. However, there was a wide assumption that he saw the handwriting on the wall and knew the white paper would eventually be cherry-picked to reinforce and amplify recommendations already made by the FRC.

Before voting the commissioners brought up the subject of affordable housing provoked by Cohen's comment: "One of the white paper's recommendations was to take a look at housing and the density that's associated with that in order to create diversity in the housing price points."[62] That was strongly urged during public comments and by the Oversight Committee in its discussions, although the word "diversity" never appeared in any of the recommendations. It was always specifically stated as either "affordable" or "workforce housing."

When asked precisely what he meant by the word "diversity" Cohen's response was: "It's a range of housing opportunities that can be affordable across the income spectrum of Collier County." Commissioner Penny Taylor then asked the question: "On the state level, is it codified? The diverse housing, is that codified?" Cohen's response was "No. It's encouraged that you have housing that meets the requirements of your community."[63]

When questioned further as to why he got rid of the word "requires" in the document, Cohen replied "... If you're going to do a 'required,' I think that starts to shut the door on those conversations where at this point all we're looking for is a framework to go forward. 'Require' or any of those kinds of mandates, if they occur, would be more appropriate in the Land Development Code, not in just a framework that you're trying to move forward with as a policy statement."[64]

By separating implementation into two tracks—the GMP amendment process and later modifications to the LDC—certain fine points could be lost in the transition and this would become one of them.

Toward the end of the meeting, Cohen made oblique reference to a series of developments that would eventually bring the Conservancy into protracted litigation against the County. It started this way: "Mr. Chair," Cohen remarked, "... if I could Commissioner, yes, we're—we have a project that's going through the process and one of the things that the white paper talks about is aggregation. As these different villages come in, how do you take a look at them as a whole to be able to address issues of conductivity, how we get more economic development, because currently you can do say, 2500 units, maybe a thousand square-foot of commercial retail, but that doesn't provide you with what I call a great technical term of the stuff to increase economic vibrancy. So as these are lined up on the runway to be able to come forward, I think this (approval) will provide us at least with the tools to be able to have that broader conversation as to how do we start to address those issues and the white paper does speak to that."

The "project" referred to was Rivergrass, and "different villages" included Longwater and Bellmar—as well as the future "aggregation" of them all into something called the Town of Big Cypress. The developer was Collier Enterprises and its various corporate subsidiaries.

The white paper did refer to "aggregation," but in a very broad sense by referencing a study done in 2001 by Dover, Kohl & Partners titled *Toward Better Places, the Community Character Plan*. The emphasis was on walkable neighborhoods, mixed use buildings, various housing types at different price points, an identifiable center and edge to communities, and special sites set aside for civic purposes. The FRC had recommended increasing village sizes to 1,500 acres, but the white paper suggested that should not happen "...unless commercial civic and governmental minimums are proposed."[65]

The Conservancy's support of the white paper was evident during public comment, as it had mustered a large number of speakers including the League of Women Voters, a long-time ally. But as the meeting wore on it became obvious that most commissioners had already made up their minds.

The final public speaker of the day was Brad Cornell representing Audubon Florida and Audubon of the Western Everglades. He was well-known to the commissioners as a thoughtful man who made low-key and sensible comments and suggestions. He had also been a member of the FRC so was familiar with the recommendations being made by Cohen and the staff. After speaking he was questioned at length by commissioners realizing that his position was basically agreeable to theirs and that his credentials as a committed environmentalist would go a long way toward neutralizing comments by the Conservancy.

When the vote was taken, Cohen's recommendations were accepted. Commissioner Solis commented: "I mean this is the way good communities work. The landowners, the groups, the environmental groups, everybody got together and came up with something, you know, that not everybody's completely happy with because everybody gave up something, but I think this is the way this process is supposed to work, and I think it's a model for how these things are supposed to happen." [66]

Town of Big Cypress

The Town of Big Cypress was not new. First proposed publicly in 2006, it was later modified as Rural Lands West during FRC deliberations and was to be partly located in a sensitive water recharge area with abundant wetlands, one of the two reasons the board and staff at the Conservancy opposed it. The other was the fact that a peer reviewed study of panther habitat had just been released, and the Conservancy knew that the latest data showed the town's location smack in the primary zone.

In its original incarnation it would be built to the east of De Soto Blvd. spreading out on both sides of Oil Well Road and contain a large shopping center with big-box stores to serve residents of Golden Gate Estates who had few shopping amenities close by. Collier Enterprises argued that it would form a sustainable tax base for further residential development with open spaces and necessary civic services, but continued to be opposed by county staff for its design of commercial activities along major roads rather than at the center of the development as with Ave Maria.

Collier Enterprises withdrew its application for Rural Lands West in January 2019. In a blistering memo it said the reason was "bureaucracy and economic overreach by Collier County management." The memo continued: "Despite the disappointing experience with the County, Collier Enterprises will continue to explore all options for pursuing investment and growth opportunities, including options outside of Collier County." And the "investment and growth opportunities" would quickly emerge a year later in the form of three new villages in the same location.

Rivergrass, Bellmar, and Longwater

Rivergrass was proposed as a "998-acre community to include up to 2,500 homes, an 18-hole bundled golf course open to the public, and 62,000 to 80,000 sq. ft. of neighborhood-scale retail and office, as well as 25,000 sq. ft. of civic, government and institutional space. New homes were anticipated to become available to homebuyers in late 2021."[67] Prices would start at $250,000, but might later vary according to the general housing market conditions in southwest Florida. Collier Enterprises indicated it would assist essential workers with down payment help.

The initial phase of the projects, originally planned to commence in 2020, would be put off until 2023. Three factors frustrated the timeline: first, a lawsuit filed by the Conservancy in 2020; second, a multi-species Habitat Conservation Plan being worked on with the United States Fish and Wildlife Service would not be completed until 2022 at the earliest; third, negotiations were underway for the sale of most Collier Enterprises assets and operations to Tarpon Blue, ". . . a Punta Gorda conglomerate . . . which owns and operates a variety of entities that focus on the acquisition and management of agricultural, development and natural resource assets across the nation."[68]

A second project planned by Collier Land Holdings was Bellmar village. Located just over one mile northwest of the National Panther Wildlife Refuge it would be slightly less than 1,000 acres with 2,750 homes and apartments, 85,000 sq. ft. of retail and office and 27,500 sq. ft. of governmental and institutional space.

The third project, located between Rivergrass and Bellmar, was Longwater. Very similar to the other two cousins, it would contain 2,600 dwelling units, 65,000 sq. ft. of retail and 25,000 sq. ft. of governmental and office space. The applicant was CDC Land Investments, another spinoff of Collier Enterprises.

The Conservancy's objections to Longwater, that it would destroy primary panther habitat, was an example of cookie-cutter development ignoring smart growth principles, and that it looked a lot more like a town than a village.

The Town of Big Cypress, after incorporating the three villages, would preserve 12,337 acres most of which bordered the western edge of the Camp Keais Strand connecting the CREW watershed to the north with the Florida Panther National Wildlife Refuge right below Bellmar. As an added benefit at build out all three villages would generate an additional $3 million for the Florida Panther Protection Fund, created by Paul Marinelli back in 2008 as an incentive

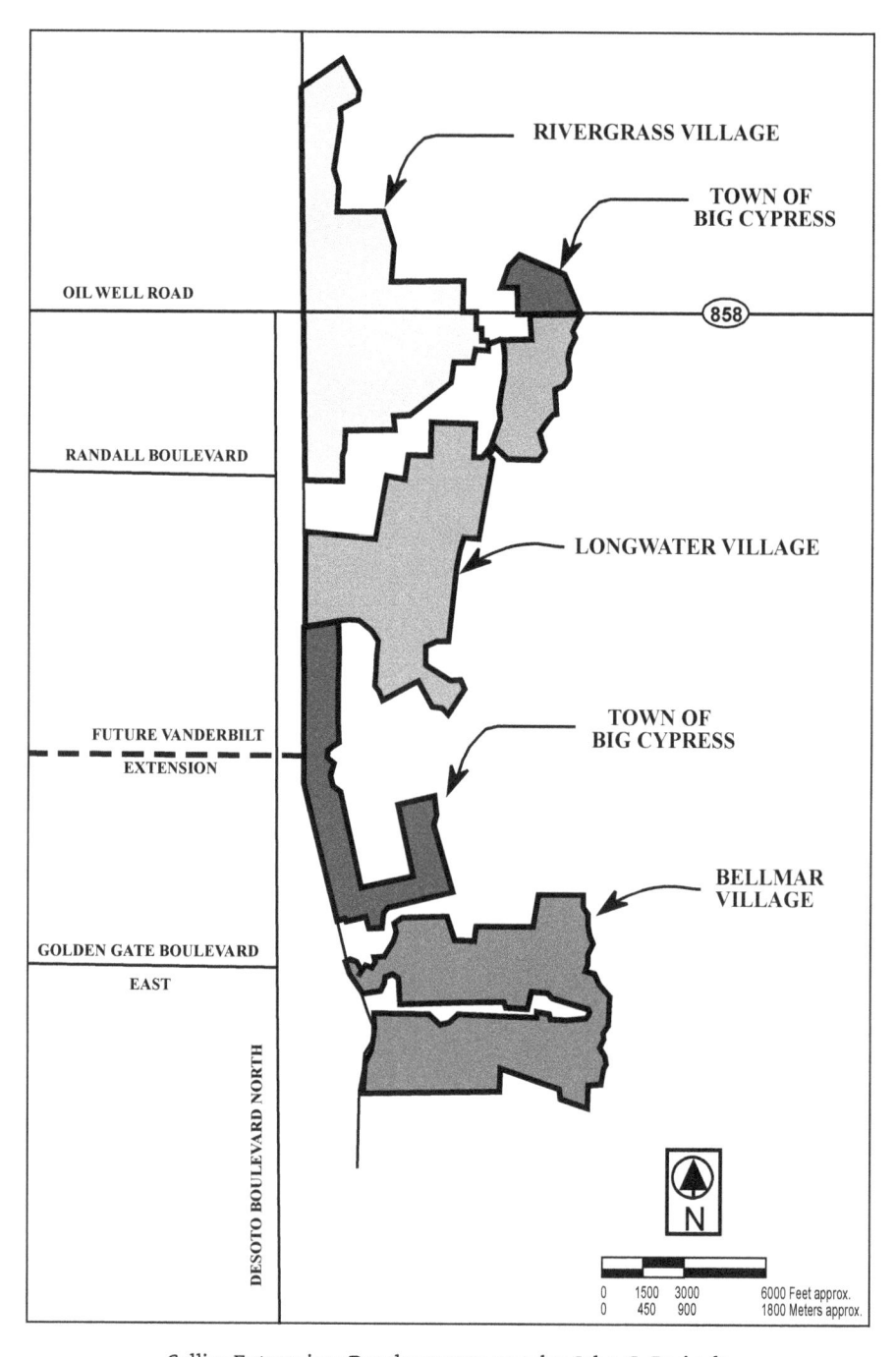

Collier Enterprises Developments map by: John G. Beriault

to encourage environmental organizations to sign on to the same agreement that the Conservancy decided to pass on.

What then came to light was a prior agreement between Collier Enterprises and the County known as "Rivergrass Village Landowner Agreement." Bottom line was that if the County Commission voted to deny Longwater and Bellmar it would amount to condemnation. County staff pointed out that if the county wanted to proceed with a highway called the Big Cypress Parkway that it should carefully think about the consequences of any failure to approve the proposed SRA's. The parkway was part of the MPO plan incorporated into an amendment, paid for by Collier Enterprises, in which the roadway's price was set at $111 million. The amendment was made in May 2018, before Collier Enterprises angrily withdrew its application for Rural Lands West. The road would be built by the developer and the agreement stated assuming Longwater and Bellmar were approved, the county would then purchase the right-of-way and the road.

The agreement appeared to put the county in a position where it would have to approve all three villages, including Rivergrass, as a package. But much of the traffic analysis was done on each of the three independently without any regard as to the cumulative impact including nearby Hyde Park Village also on track for permitting.

This package approval was further evidence, according to the Conservancy, that the plan was really for a town, not just three independent villages. And the difference was substantial. Towns had minimal space requirements for goods and services, civic and governmental buildings, and community parks. The combined plan for the three villages fell way short of what would be needed in a single town of 7,850 dwelling units.

The Conservancy also noted that written into a February 2020 draft memo reviewing Longwater that the following sentence appeared: "Comprehensive Planning staff also asked that the departments and agencies involved directly with the Concurrency Management give consideration to the cumulative effects or demands of these SRA, rather than considering each only individually." When the memo was issued in final version that statement was redacted.

To accommodate anticipated growth with the necessary infrastructure such as water, sewer and storm water management, Collier Enterprises had created the Big Cypress Stewardship District based on the Ave Maria model.

In a parallel move, the County created the Northeast Utilities Facility District to provide both potable and wastewater treatment to existing subdivisions in the same area. "It purchased land to site the Northeast Utility Facilities in June 2003 and approved the design of these facilities in 2004. The designs were completed in 2010; however, a decline in population growth put the program on hold until reactivated by the Board in 2017."[69] To do so, a $334 million bond issue was authorized, amortized by a 27% increase in fees for sewer and water from customers of existing subdivisions like Twin Eagles, Orange Blossom

Ranch and Valencia Golf and Country Club, and fees later collected on future build out.

That relieved the developers of a major up-front financial obligation, but Judy Hushon, a long-time board member of the Conservancy, was appalled. She was convinced that the projected collections would not offset the cost of debt service. The difference would end up as higher fees and taxes levied on county residents. Her argument was that occupancy assumptions for the new villages were too low. She concluded that "... developers estimate 54,000 total residents but, based on the FDOT estimates, actual build-out will probably generate over 80,000 residents. As a result, the county will need to construct additional infrastructure at additional cost to the taxpayer."[70]

Lawsuit Against Rivergrass

Looking at documents submitted for approval of the three villages comprising the Town of Big Cypress, both Nicole Johnson and April Olson were struck by the fact that of the three, Rivergrass was the most poorly planned. Using the principles of smart growth from the 2001 Dover, Kohl & Partners report, instead of being walkable and bikeable, and having a central area as a gathering place for retail and commercial, Rivergrass would be bisected by a four-lane high-speed highway effectively splitting the community in half.[71]

According to the Collier County MPO 2040 Long Range Transportation Plan (LRTP) 800 trucks a day traveled along

Oil Well Road carrying everything from mining materials to agricultural products. The speed limit at the time on the two-lane road was 55 mph, but the County's 2019–2023 work program intended to widen Oil Well to six lanes. The village center was planned for the south side of the highway making it daunting for those who lived north of the road to get to shops and restaurants. The location of the retail area may have been left over from the earliest version of the Town of Big Cypress where the plan was for big-box stores. While the problem was the same as one that concerned County staff and held up approval of the earlier version of Rural Lands West, it was now a new era with a new commission and a commitment to growth at any cost.

The Conservancy realized that it was alone, but had been there before. After threatening litigation over the design of Pelican Bay, it had worked as a partner with Westinghouse to take advantage of the natural amenities provided by Clam Bay and fringing mangrove forests. There was a faint hope that this might happen again, but after careful deliberation the decision was made to file suit against Collier County for violating terms of the GMP and LDC. Rob Moher knew that the case would be complex. In his mind, the entire future of the eastern lands depended heavily upon the county's strict adherence to the terms of the GMP and LDC. And he knew that Collier Enterprises would enter the suit soon after it was filed.

In a later conversation, as Moher reflected upon the lawsuit he said: "It really wasn't about the eastern lands or the rural lands. Those words have little meaning to a lot of people new to southwest Florida. It really was about the western Everglades. It really was about the whole drainage system and aquifer recharge areas. It really was about the Camp Keais and Okaloacoochee Slough. It's about much more than that."

Rivergrass bordered a wetland to the east, as did Longwater and Bellmar. It was Camp Keais Slough, an important recharge area for Collier County flowing into the Big Cypress National Preserve and designated as an FSA for high level of protection. Plans were to use it as a buffer against the incursion of wild animals into the subdivisions.

A Bit of History

The Conservancy and Collier Enterprises were no strangers in the court of law. In 1986, the company filed an application to begin processing the Villages of Sable Bay. The subdivision was planned with 4,000 dwelling units, 45 holes of golf and hotels. The entire footprint would cover 2,200 acres running from Thomasson Drive, south along US 41 with an extension eastward all the way to Naples Bay for what would become a yacht fueling and docking facility called Hamilton Harbor. The harbor project was in the city and the residential and commercial in the county. Dredge and fill had already ripped out over half of the mangroves in the bay and the Conservancy's concern was mainly with the coastal part of the development and led to a suit filed with Florida Audubon alleging that the county commission had approved the county's portion of the project without the mandatory environmental impact statement. In 1989, an administrative law judge ruled in favor of the plaintiffs.

As the case worked its way through the appellate process, the Collier company attempted to use pressure from Tallahassee to push the project through until August 2003 when it announced an option agreement for WCI communities to take over Sabal Bay. It was a smart ploy. WCI had developed Pelican Bay with the Conservancy as a partner and announced reduced housing units in Sabal Bay while offering to improve the Lely Canal (which Collier Development had already done) bisecting the proposed project.[72]

The Hamilton Harbor Yacht Club, being mostly in the city, was on a different track. The company managed to gin up some support from the Naples City Council in 1999 to rezone the area around Hamilton Harbor, an act followed immediately by a lawsuit filed by Citizens to Preserve Naples Bay and other conservation groups. The Conservancy's president David Guggenheim believed he could make a deal that would prevent adverse effects on the bay but the board overruled its president and decided to join the suit.

Guggenheim persisted but it never worked out. After some months of back and forth it was obvious settlement negotiations were going nowhere and the city had no interest in attempting to move the parties along. Eventually an agreement was reached in 2003 by Kathy Prosser, the new president of the Conservancy, and Tom Flood, significantly reducing the size of the marina and getting 30 acres of mangrove mitigation

Then, the real estate market began to soften. WCI pulled out of its option agreement and in 2011 Collier Enterprises sold the development rights to Minto Corporation, a Canadian company known for its environmental sensitivity. It went on to build the Isles of Collier's Reserve creating a pedestrian friendly community, respecting wetlands and embodying most of the principles of smart growth.

Theory of the Case

As Johnson and Olson reviewed the Rivergrass plan they became convinced that three areas had not been adequately addressed in accordance with the terms of the existing growth management plan: excavating and building in primary panther habitat, inadequate housing diversity and an opaque and an erroneous analysis of the cost to the taxpayer of the project's infrastructure violating a state and county requirement known as fiscal neutrality.

With the board's support, Moher engaged Brian Israel, lead attorney of the Environmental Practice Group at Arnold & Porter, a Washington-based firm. Israel had been the lead attorney in the BP *Deepwater Horizon* litigation. He had served in the U.S. Department of Justice before moving to private practice, and participated in a number of other high-profile suits involving corporations running afoul of environmental laws. He was plainspoken and capable of translating complex legal issues into layman's language.

Florida Panther

As Israel prepared the case, he knew the argument on the panther was going to be the toughest. While over 70% of Rivergrass Village site was located in the primary zone, the cats' population had clearly increased during the previous two decades since the first RLSA overlay was adopted in 2002, confirmed by landowners such as Leisa Priddy who, along with her husband, was the third-largest owner in the rural lands.

The crux of his argument would be that the language of the overlay was specific in its intent to "... direct incompatible uses away from wetlands and upland habitat." The statute creating the Rural Lands Stewardship Act stated that SRAs should "... avoid conflict with significant environmentally sensitive areas resources and habitats."[73] That required preservation of open spaces where telemetry data showed high levels of panther activity. But a counterargument continued to be hammered home by Florida Wildlife Federation and Florida Audubon, actively promoting Paul Marinelli's panther protection program funded by landowner fees to be used for wildlife corridors and road underpasses. The Conservancy's sharp critique was always blunted by other environmental organizations dedicated entirely to wildlife and habitat preservation.

Housing Diversity

One of the arguments raging in southwest Florida at the time was the lack of affordable housing. The GMOC had studied the subject extensively and Van Lengen had concluded the best way to ensure workforce housing was through increased density. The Conservancy suit pointed out that the current ratio of housing types and Collier County was about 50% single family and 45% multifamily, with the remaining 5% primarily mobile homes, but in Rivergrass 90% of the housing units would be single-family. More expensive to build and more expensive to buy.

Fiscal Neutrality

The third part of the complaint was clearer cut. The company had engaged Development Planning and Financial Group (DPFG) as its consultant to prove fiscal neutrality. Among the base assumptions was a population estimate of 1.71 people per housing unit. However, DPFG did not provide the methodology for the calculation, which was below the normal range of 2.5 to 2.8 per household in Collier County. The Conservancy challenged this estimate since it formed the basis for all the infrastructure needed to serve the village, particularly as Rivergrass was planned for 90% single family homes. In fact, Collier Enterprises consultant's economic assessment stated that single-family homes housed many more school-age children than multifamily buildings. The contradiction was obvious and blatant, hurricane flags were flying and the Conservancy was convinced that Rivergrass Village would never become fiscally neutral.

In the Courts

The suit was filed in early March 2020 in the 20th District Court of Florida. The Conservancy asked the court to overturn the development order based upon violations of the county's GMP; the case was assigned to Judge Lauren Brodie.

Two months later, as the county was preparing its defense, Collier Enterprises Management (CEM) joined as an intervenor, accompanied by a news release touting the company's environmental preservation set asides, mainly 5,250 acres of land for preservation to the east of the development along the Camp Keais Slough. It was represented by Stearns Weaver Miller, a large firm with offices throughout Florida.

The Conservancy subsequently amended its complaint by removing a section about panther habitat being destroyed by the development, saying it was due to the need to protect all native wildlife. The amendment went on to emphasize the importance of federal agency reviews.

The County and CEM then filed a response arguing that the Conservancy lacked standing to file the suit because it had "no specific knowledge as to the potential risks to wildlife posed by Rivergrass. In fact, Plaintiff admits it has not done 'any sort of analysis of the expected injury to wildlife specific to the Rivergrass development,' nor 'identified any characteristics of Rivergrass that make it more or less likely for development to cause injury to wildlife.'"[74]

In a second motion, this one for summary judgment, CEM's' lawyers argued that the Conservancy "brought the wrong claims, in the wrong proceeding, and through the wrong vehicle."[75]

A hearing on the first motion was scheduled for December 17 before Judge Brodie, and on the second motion December 21. Both would be virtual due to the COVID virus' prevalence at the time.

Those hearings never took place. In a move that raised a few eyebrows, Judge Brodie resigned from the case and was replaced by Judge Hugh Hayes, a long-time member of the court looking to soon retire. In order to process the facts of the case he rescheduled the hearing and trial dates from December to May 2021. A strict constitutionalist, Hayes had been appointed to the Circuit Court by Gov. Bob Graham in 1982 and would later retire in January 2023.

The Conservancy's case was heard over a five-day period with much of the testimony from two expert witnesses: Robert Minnicozzi a member of the American Institute of Certified Planners (AICP) and Charles Gauthier, also a fellow of the AICP who had four years' service as planning manager for Collier County from 1985 to 1989.

In his decision, Judge Hayes quickly dismissed Minnicozzi's testimony as to the design of Rivergrass. "The court finds that: (a) Mr. Minnicozzi lacked an understanding of the key issues of this case relating to use, density, and intensity of use; (b) Mr. Minnicozzi's opinions are contrary to, and at times ignore, the plain language of the GMP; and

(c) Mr. Minnicozzi's testimony is not credible; accordingly, the court gives his opinions minimal weight."[76]

Gauthier's testimony was to critique design of the village in terms of pedestrian and bicycle circulation and interconnectivity. However, he admitted that many of the design elements he was talking about were in fact not included in the GMP. With that Judge Hayes ruled: "In the end, Mr. Gauthier's opinions rest upon the omission of keywords from the GMP and the addition of words and requirements that do not exist in the GMP; accordingly, the court gives his opinions minimal weight."[77]

The main witness for CEM and the county was Robert Mulhere, from Hole and Montes, an engineering firm. Giving extensive testimony it was the judge's opinion that "... in addition to effectively rebutting Mr. Minnicozzi and Mr. Gauthier, Mr. Mulhere gave clear and convincing expert opinion testimony that the Development Order is consistent with the use, density, and intensity of use requirements of the GMP." Hayes continued: "the court does not believe it necessary to rely on expert opinion in order to determine consistency here; rather, the Court need only independently compare the plain text of the Development Order to the plain text of the GMP. However, upon balancing the credibility and weight of the expert opinions at trial, the court credits the opinions of Mr. Mulhere and finds that his testimony supports the court's independent conclusions below with respect to the development orders consistency with the GMP."[78]

The judge's ruling was: "Defendants have met their burden and have established that the development order is consistent with the GMP as it pertains to use, density and intensity of use; plaintiff has failed to introduce any evidence that would warrant a contrary finding."[79]

The court then retained jurisdiction with regard to attorney's fees and costs relating to any matter in the execution of the judgment issued. The loser had to pay the prevailing party's attorney's fees according to Florida law, despite the fact that the Conservancy's counsel disagreed with the premises upon which the law was based.

The Appeal

Disappointed by the decision, the Conservancy had an ace in the hole. It was a case in north Florida titled *Imhoff vs Walton*. A three-judge panel in the First District Court of Appeals had issued an opinion in September 2021 reversing the trial court's ruling for a developer. The appellate court sided with residents and two local environmental organizations, rejecting a trial judge's decision that local comprehensive plans could only be challenged by asserting that density, intensity and use were the only relevant sections that could be cited. The case was right on point, because Judge Hayes had failed to allow the Conservancy to present its case on the Florida panther, traffic and particularly fiscal neutrality.

"In the Walton County case, the panel of three appellate judges stated that 'the trial court should have considered all their claims of inconsistency' because *all* rules of the comprehensive plan matter," said Nicole Johnson. "This is encouraging as the Walton County ruling increases the likelihood that the Second District will likewise reverse the trial court's ruling on Rivergrass."[80]

And it did.

In its decision the court stated: "The question we address here is whether the Conservancy's claims concerning the traffic and fiscal impacts of the Rivergrass Village development could be brought within the ambit of a section 163.3215 action. The circuit court concluded that they couldn't. We disagree. We are compelled to reverse that aspect of the judgment below and remand for further proceedings."[81]

The court affirmed the density, intensity and land use part of Hayes' decision, but also said that he "went too far" when he did not allow, the Conservancy's arguments that expected traffic and fiscal impacts from Rivergrass violated the county's own GMP: "On that discrete issue, we find there were disputed material facts which precluded summary judgment."[82]

Both sides took to the media with a positive spin. In a statement to the local press, Christian Spilker, president and CEO of Collier Enterprises and a partner at Tarpon Blue Family of Companies, said the ruling "cleared the way for work to begin on Rivergrass Village by reaffirming a lower court's decision that the project is consistent with Collier County's comprehensive plan."[83] The Conservancy had a different take, claiming that it would have its day in court on excluded areas of discovery. Judge Hayes had announced his retirement and a new judge would be assigned, creating a degree of uncertainty in how the case might be tried.

The standoff held all parties at bay until June of 2023 when settlement discussions began among lawyers for the two sides, and on July 15, 2023, an agreement was reached.

The Conservancy was sanguine about the terms: "First, Collier Enterprises has agreed to permanently preserve 655 acres of primary panther habitat through a conservation easement granted to the Conservancy. For purposes of scale, this 655-acre parcel consists of nearly the same acreage of primary panther habitat that is within the site of Rivergrass Village. Furthermore, this parcel is strategically located between Golden Gate Estates and the Florida Panther National Wildlife Refuge, which will permanently protect important habitat that is part of a critical corridor connection between the two areas.

"Second, as a part of our settlement, Collier Enterprises has committed to extinguish 65,000 development credits as part of their sale of land to the State of Florida for the Caloosahatchee Big Cypress Corridor, funded during the 2023 Florida Legislative Session. This reduction of credits will significantly reduce the overall development potential for the entire RLSA by 6,500 acres, which is an area greater than six villages the size of the 1,000-acre Rivergrass. The Conservancy believes that this reduction in the RLSA's overall development footprint will result in fewer impacts to habitats, additional agricultural lands and wetlands saved, and an overall reduction in future traffic within the region.

"The Conservancy's Board, members, and supporters stood by the Conservancy throughout this lengthy, yet important, three-year challenge. Thirteen civic and environmental organizations filed amicus briefs in support of the Conservancy's appeal, including: Center for Biological Diversity, Sierra Club Florida, Strong Towns, League of Women Voters of Collier County, Florida Rights of Nature Network, Sanibel-Captiva Conservation Foundation, Calusa Waterkeeper, Environmental Confederation of Southwest Florida, Cypress Cove Landkeepers, Stone Crab Alliance, Golden Gate Estates Area Civic Association, Friends of the Everglades, and Tropical Audubon Society represented by the Everglades Law Center."[84]

CEM and Tarpon Blue were more restrained in their comments, but pleased that they could now begin construction on Rivergrass and the other two villages with no legal encumbrances. Finally, both sides agreed to pay their own legal fees which had run into millions of dollars.

The Conservancy felt the settlement was fair but that it had diverted a great deal of attention away from what was happening throughout both Lee and Collier counties. With the FRC plan in place in Collier a flood of new developments were in the pipeline for permitting, and Lee County was running at an even faster clip.

Hyde Park Village

In June 2020, the County Commission heard an application for Hyde Park (later rebranded) consisting of 642 acres with 1,800 homes, and anywhere between 300 and 1,000 multifamily units located west of Everglades Boulevard and north of Oil Well Road. It would feature 45,000 sq. ft. of commercial space, and 18,000 sq. ft. for government, civic and institutional uses as well as a possible medical facility. At less than 700 acres, commissioners felt it was more manageable than the villages in the Town of Big Cypress. The development plan had a price point beginning at $168,000 for multifamily units but cautioned that was a function of market conditions and could change at any time. The Conservancy's April Olson noted that the project avoided primary panther habitat and was located near existing developed areas, but she was concerned about the construction of a strip mall along Oil Well Road to the south and the developer's mushy commitment to affordable housing.

County staff recommended that the developer make a firm commitment to build a minimum of 215 units in the "... low, moderate and affordability ranges. This is a market rate development that right now is proposing to hit the lower end of the market," Cormac Giblin, the county's housing and grant development manager told commissioners. But market conditions could change, he said, "so the staff recommendation is to ensure that a minimum number of those units actually wind up being built and that they commit to a small percentage of what they are already saying they will do as part of the approval process."[85] Never happened.

Immokalee Road Rural Village

In February 2021 one of the larger projects came before the county's planning commission. Brought by a Palm Beach company partially owned by billionaire developer Jeff Greene, it was a request for a GMP amendment and rezone of a little over 2,700 acres, of which 585 were in SSAs and 211 in Neutral Lands. The applicant intended to build about 4,000 housing units accompanied by 350,000 sq. ft. of retail and 100,000 sq. ft. of office and other commercial space.[86] It would be located east of Immokalee Road, in the Rural Fringe, and smack in the eastern terminus of the Corkscrew Regional Ecosystem Watershed (CREW), one of the most sensitive environmental areas in Lee and Collier counties. Done badly, it would directly impact Audubon's famous Corkscrew Swamp Sanctuary.

Designation as a "village" was a bit mistaken because the developed area would be nearly 2,000 acres and the GMP and LDC allowed villages to be no more than 1,000 acres. The difference between a "village" and a "town" was significant in that the latter required increased amenities and services for residents, but if a rezone could be accomplished it would relieve the developer of those responsibilities and added costs.

The project had a long and somewhat checkered history. In order to have vehicle access, an entry would need to be cut at two-lane Immokalee Road before the bend leading to Corkscrew Swamp Sanctuary, then run through the subdivision and out again to the north on Immokalee after it turned east. In order to do this the developer had to purchase land from County Commissioner William McDaniel—land where his excavating company site was located. And McDaniel knew Jeff Greene, who had contributed to his

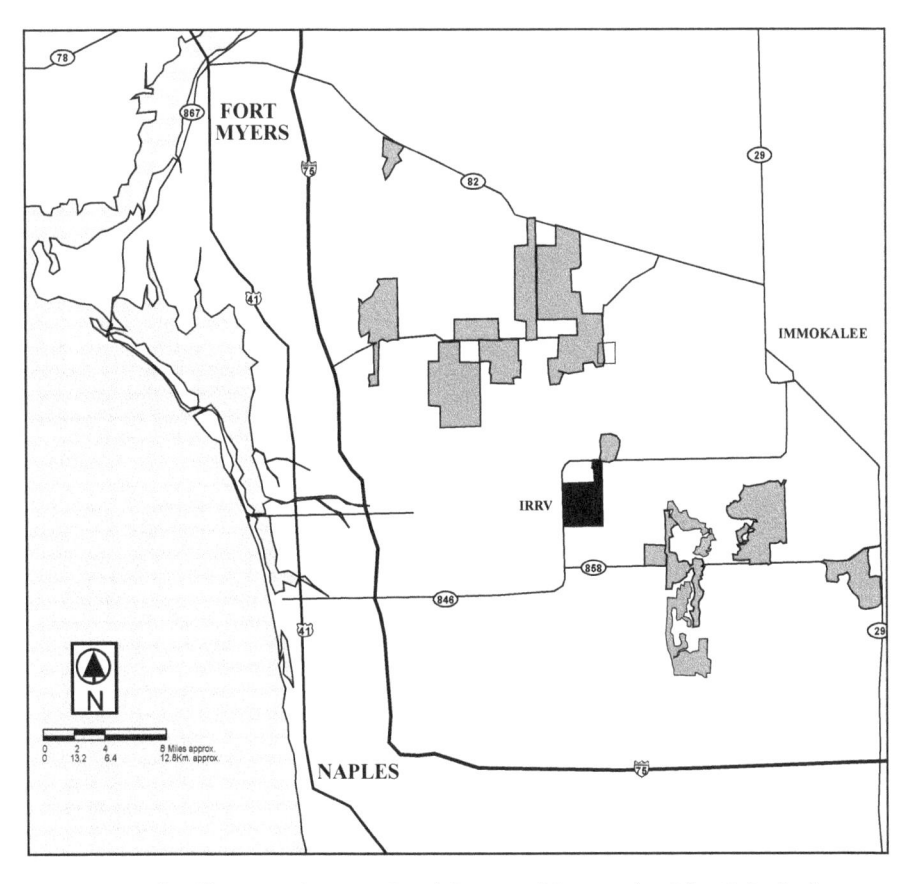

Lee and Collier Counties New Gated Communities map by: John G. Beriault

2016 campaign. In a series of dazzling transactions, the commissioner ended up selling the property and being forgiven $42.7 million for defaulted loans as part of the complicated deal.[87]

McDaniel's vote at the commission hearing was necessary for a growth management plan amendment because it required a super majority. He consulted with the county attorney to receive clearance to participate based on the fact that he was no longer involved in any part of the project.

At the hearing, petitioner's representative Bob Mulhere of Hole Montes, told the commission that some environmental organizations, the same ones signed on to the rural lands' memorandum of agreement with ECPO, were working with the developer to mitigate effects on the wildlife and bird population in the area. With the project being built around a quarry, Greene also wanted to reduce the littoral zone by 50% and offered to offset that loss with plantings around bordering lakes scattered about the village. A few environmental objections were mildly raised and the project was approved 4-1 with McDaniel voting for transmittal to other agencies for their review.

However, to the chagrin of lawyers accustomed to getting their own way, commissioners held the line on the rezone, realizing that by increasing acres within a village to 1,998 would constitute precedent, and that was a little further than they wanted to go at the time.

In a 13-page letter, Amber Crooks, the Conservancy's Environmental Policy Manager, and Jessica Wilson, Senior

Water Quality Specialist, blasted the IRRV permit application. They pointed out that the neighboring CREW, with 60,000 acres provided "... flood protection, where filtration, and aquifer recharge for the County's drinking water supplies as well as crucial habitat and wildlife corridors."[88] Two hundred acres of wetlands could be destroyed and partially filled along with other surface waters. Their comments went on to point out that there were a series of inconsistencies between submissions to government agencies by the developer, and that the overall project could result in a net loss of wetlands while the mitigation plan submitted indicated there would be a net gain. Since almost 600 acres were in Sending Areas, the project also overlaid primacy panther habitat, and impacted foraging areas for both the endangered Crested Caracara and wood storks nesting in Corkscrew Swamp Sanctuary less than 2 miles away.

The Conservancy letter was addressed to FDEP but to confirm its continued opposition made the point in the letter that by sending it "... does not constitute support for the state assumed section 404 permitting program, which we believe is unlawful."[89] The letter also reflected in increasing concern with the impact of developments on the CREW and on Lee County's Density Reduction/Groundwater Recharge area. The Conservancy's policy team, while maintaining that the transfer the state was unlawful, had to deal with the rapid processing of 404 permits by overwhelmed staff at FDEP resulting in incomplete analysis of both immediate and cumulative effects of development.

Lee County and CREW

In late 1990, the Florida Land Acquisition Advisory Council (LAAC) decided to add almost 50,000 acres in Lee and Collier County to the Conservation and Recreation Lands (CARL) priority list. The purpose was to connect a series of conservation areas into contiguous habitat and to protect the water flowing from the area around Audubon's Corkscrew Swamp Sanctuary into the Fakahatchee and Florida Panther National Wildlife Refuge. The main flow way would be the Camp Keais Strand. The preserved area would be managed by the South Florida Water Management District (SFWMD).

The proposed project was quickly boosted into reality by Ben Hill Griffin, Sr. His company, Alico, had 4,600 acres on the upper end of the CREW boundary and he had a desire to see his land protected to be used for hiking and recreation. Offered at a fair price, when the first purchase took place it was actually 6,700 acres, all from Alico.

In 1992 the LAAC amended the design of the project to allow matching funds to come from Lee County and the SFWMD. The Pepper Ranch, 2,500 acres, was purchased by Conservation Collier in 2009 and by 2020 over 55,000 acres had been purchased into either public ownership or control by a land trust.

In addition to protecting contiguous habitat and the Camp Keais flow way, the CREW overlays Lee County's

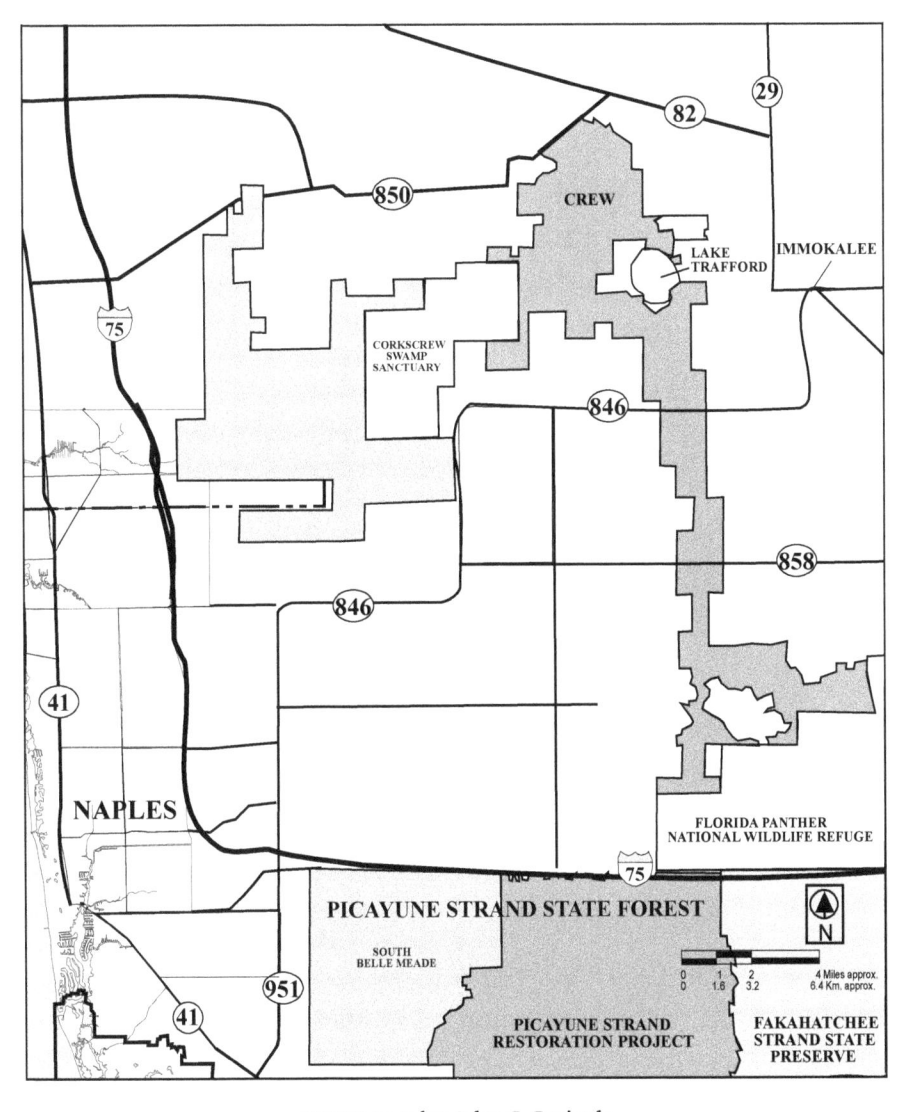

CREW map by: John G. Beriault

Density Reduction/Groundwater Recharge (DR/GR), the main source aquifer replenishment for a part of Lee County. The DR/GR had been under attack by mining and development companies for years and that is what the next chapter is all about.

Corkscrew Road Builds Up

Immokalee Road runs from US 41 east through Collier County where it swings north just past the 7,000-acre Bird Rookery Swamp, part of the CREW, and then again turns east at the entry road leading to Corkscrew Swamp Sanctuary. It continues across the 16,600-acre Camp Keais Strand and eventually into the town of Immokalee.

To the north, the next major east-west is Corkscrew Road. From I-75 it runs northeast, is joined by Alico Road then runs east past Corkscrew Marsh and into SR 82. The highway is fringed on both sides by a series of cookie-cutter gated communities.

A number of smaller subdivisions, including Grandezza and Stoneybrook, had been built along Corkscrew Road before it connected with Alico Road, but after the 2008–2009 housing recession abated, permitting for new developments took off. The first new community on the road from Estero was Wild Blue opening in 2018. Accessible through guarded gates from Corkscrew Road on the south and Alico on the north, it has four lakes on lots with small houses surrounding the ponds. Over 3,000 acres, 800 being lakes, and 1,100 new homes it promotes itself as a "British West

Indies styled community, the brilliant collaboration between recognized builders, including Lennar, WCI and Stock Development."[90] It was the first of a series of developments by Cameratta Companies.

A second subdivision was The Place—1,300 acres with 700 being wetlands and constructed natural areas. It was platted for almost 1,300 homes at the upper end of the price scale to be built by national companies like Lennar and Pulte and quickly sold out.

Further east and on the south side of Corkscrew Road lies Verdana Village, a Cameratta Companies development with

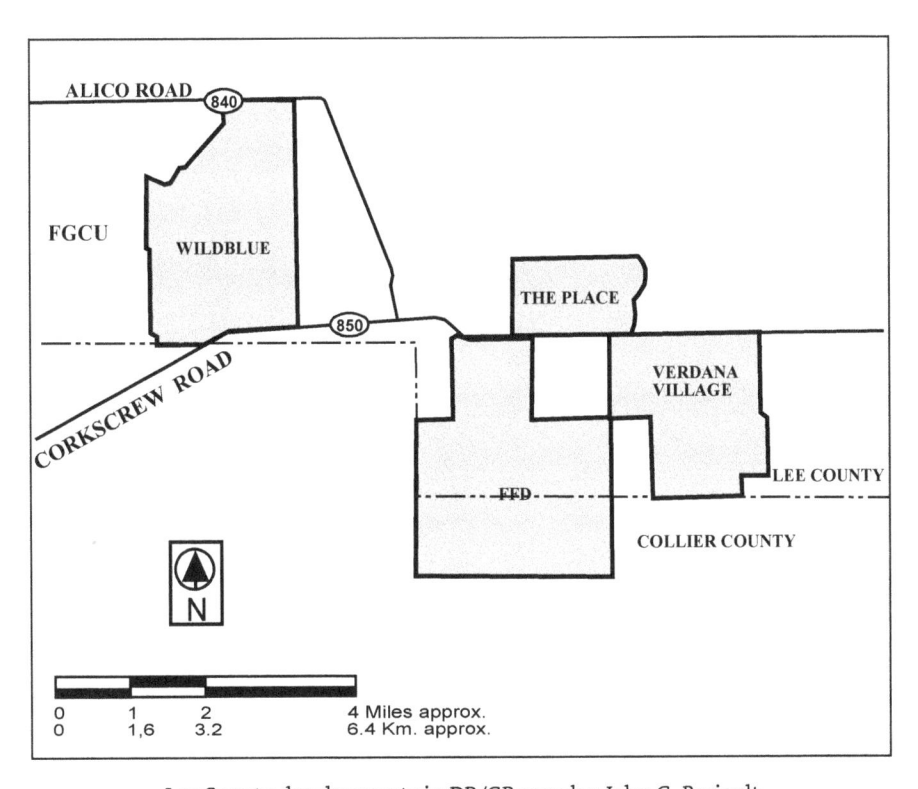

Lee County developments in DR/GR map by: John G. Beriault

Pulte and Lennar building single family homes ranging from $500,000-$1 million. Residents were promised athletic facilities, swimming pools and a shopping center right outside its gates with over 70,000 sq. ft. of retail space.

Each of the aforementioned communities destroyed a small part of the ecosystem and altered hydrology but the developers always promised to make some attempt to both restore and enhance water flow. The quality of that flow was a different matter, but the argument always was that row crop agriculture used herbicides, fertilizers and pesticides and a carefully controlled development was a better alternative.

The real impact was about to come, in the form of a trio of large prospective developments. All would be built in sensitive land in the DR/GR and all would eventually have an impact on Audubon's Corkscrew Swamp Sanctuary and its wildlife. And all would bring the Conservancy into an aggressive posture in insisting that permitting be full, fair and complete. We will now turn to the still unfolding story of the three: Troyer Mine, Florida Farms Development and Kingston.

DR/GR

In southeastern Lee County lies a massive area called the Density Reduction/Groundwater Resource area. Established in the early 1990s at over 81,000 acres, it provides nearly 70% of Lee County's potable water and is habitat for a number of endangered and threatened species including the Florida panther. With no particular priority assigned to specific sections, it was intended to have low density housing of one unit per 10 acres, lime rock mining, agriculture and conservation land, but each of the first three would require a rezone.

Water flow in the DR/GR is generally from the northeast to southwest. In the westernmost third, most ends up in the Estero River and Estero Bay. In the central portion, it oozes down the Flint Pen Strand of the CREW and eventually into Bird Rookery Strand and the Cocohatchee River. The eastern portion feeds into Corkscrew Swamp Sanctuary and eventually into the Camp Keais Strand in Collier County. Taken as a whole, water from the DR/GR nourishes critical watershed flow ways all the way down into the Florida National Panther Wildlife Preserve, the Fakahatchee Strand and the Big Cypress.

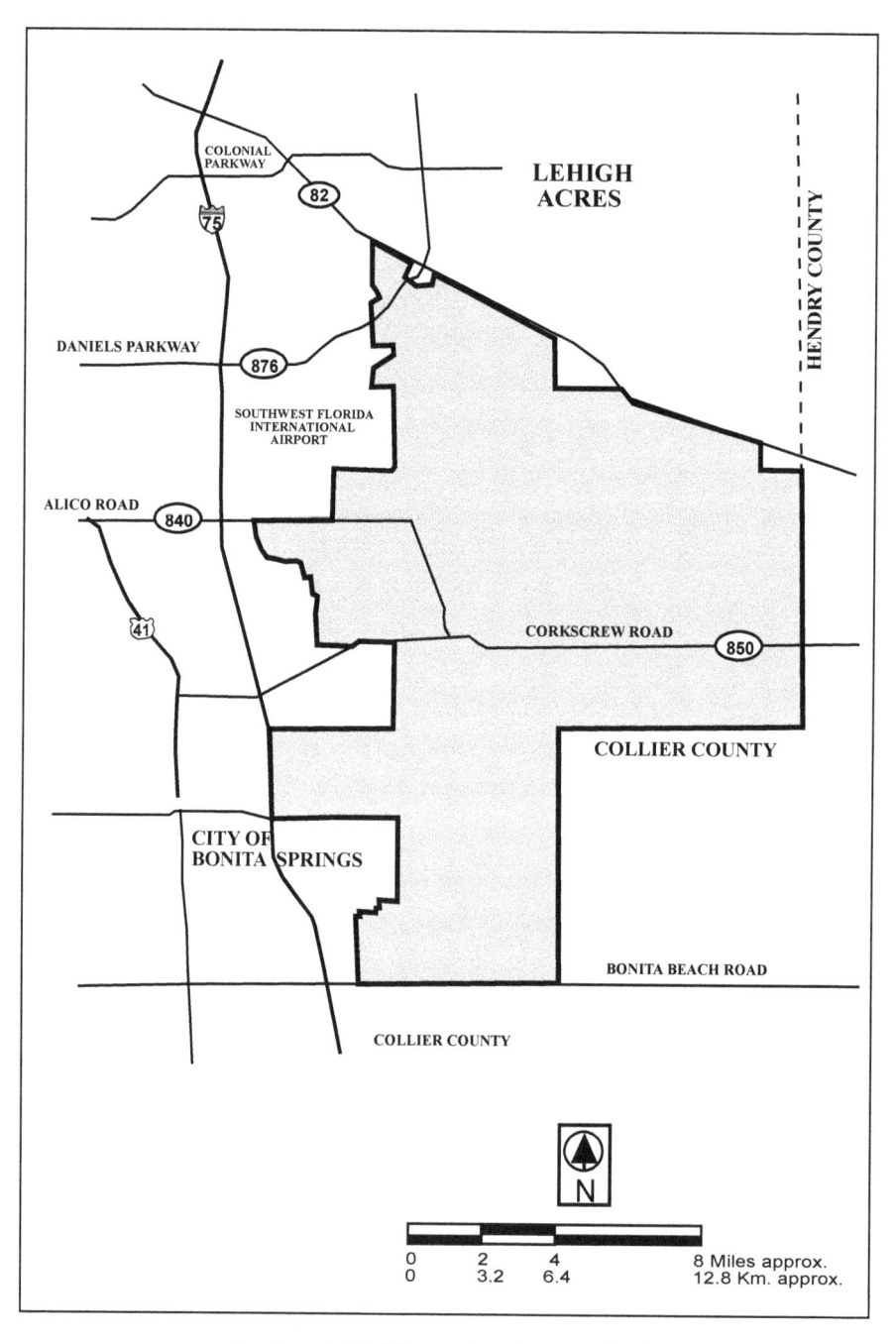

Lee County DR/GR map by: John G. Beriault

In 2003 a Lee County committee recommended review of groundwater sources, potable wellfield protection and mining, driven by the fact that Estero Bay had been designated as "impaired." The bay was an important asset. It was Florida's first designated Aquatic Preserve. With parks along the shore and popular beaches, it was clear that land uses would require significant modification and remediation to bring the bay into conformity with the Total Maximum Daily Load (TMDL) calculated to clean up the water. Adding to the pressure to take a hard look at the DR/GR was the number of applications pending for new mines.

In response County staff prepared a set of recommendations, and after public hearings and despite the fact that no parties at interest were completely satisfied, the County Commission adopted the new plan.

Land along major east-west arterials like Corkscrew Road and Alico Road was designated as appropriate for mixed use communities so long as they remain outside natural resource areas. Other sections along Alico Road, where rock mining had historically occurred, were identified as most suitable for future mining activity. To obtain a degree of formality and common understanding, an overlay known as Map 14 was created and adopted in 2010. Immediately challenged by mining companies, it was upheld in 2012 by an Administrative Law Judge.

Once the 2008–2009 housing crisis abated demand picked up and landowners along Corkscrew Road began to create specific site plans for their properties. The county allowed increased density in exchange for benefits beyond the limitations of existing zoning. But as was so common in southwest Florida at the time, a number of the projects never fulfilled the standards, some even expanding overlays and adding in commercial development—never part of the original plan. By doing so Map 14 was conveniently ignored and by 2017 Lee County staff, with a new and eager County Commission, decided to simply do away with the overlay.

Getting Rid of Map 14

The initial attempt was to do it quietly with little notice and no public meetings, but it was quickly abandoned and a more formal process put in place working through the local planning agency and ultimately, in early 2019, to the Lee County Board of Commissioners.

The Conservancy was all over it. "Lee County's responsibility is to protect the interests of Lee County citizens. Map 14 and its supporting policies do this by directing impactful activities such as mining to a specific area while allowing for a process that engages private landowners and the public in new mining needs to be added, as well as requiring a needs assessment to verify that additional lime rock supply is necessary. Map 14 has been one of the successful ways Lee County has protected and managed competing and incompatible interests and uses in the DR/GR. The Conservancy is urging Lee County commission to retain Map 14 and associated ... policies."[91]

The county's planning staff was fully engaged in the debate as it rolled into the early summer of 2019, putting out a series of questions and answers supporting the move to abandon Map 14. The Conservancy and the Village of Estero sliced and diced staff arguments but commissioners paid little heed and voted 3 to 1 to wipe out the overlay.

Cumulative Impacts

Dismissing Map 14 also had the effect of validating a number of developments along Corkscrew Road beginning construction or in the process of permitting. They included Wild Blue, Verdana Village and The Place.

But there were three in the eastern part of the DR/GR where the environmental impacts would be magnified: a lime rock mine and two large proposed developments sitting right on top of, and adjacent to, Audubon's Corkscrew Swamp Sanctuary flow way. That is now where we will now turn to examine the extent and long-term cumulative effects of the three on the delicate ecosystem of the CREW and Corkscrew Swamp with particular emphasis on two: Florida Farms Development and Kingston.

Saga of the Troyer Mine

Troyer Brothers property stretches 5.6 miles from SR 82 south down to Corkscrew Road, bordered on both sides by conservation land, some of which had been bought by Lee 20/20. For years, it had been used for potato farming, and just to the north of the property was Sakata Seed America's

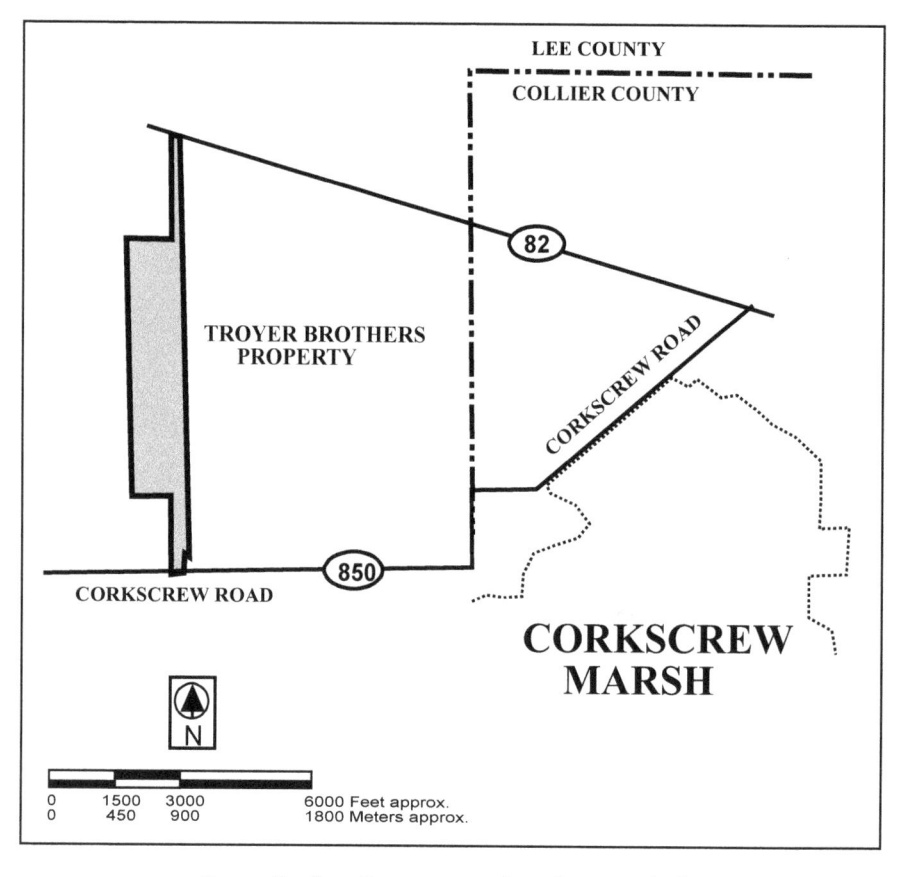

Troyer Brothers Property map by: John G. Beriault

research facility, dedicated to experiments in various fruit and vegetable seed hybrids.

In 2009, Troyer requested a rezone of its land for mining but was rejected by both a hearing examiner and Lee County commission, based partly on the fact that it was not within the traditional Alico Road mining corridor. Even more daunting was a Corps of Engineers proposal to do an environmental review under the National Environmental

Policy Act (NEPA). The Corps would, in its review, likely study the impact of mining on all federal wetlands, and this possibility gave Lee County officials heartburn, causing a hard stop to any further consideration.

Then, during the latter days of the Trump administration, Troyer Brothers resubmitted its application. By the summer of 2019, it was ready for commission approval and submission to the Department of Economic Opportunity in Tallahassee and federal permitting authorities. Criteria was a matter of determining the need for, and availability of, additional lime rock supply in South Florida, analysis of the mining location in terms of transportation facilities and impacts, compatibility with adjacent land uses, a review of wildlife and endangered and threatened species, and finally the impact on groundwater, surface water and water quality as it might affect nearby wellfields and recharge. This last was important because the DR/GR contains four major Lee County utility wellfields as well as one for Bonita Springs.

Lee County staff had a problem. With Map 14 about to be eliminated, they had to be cautious in how they handled applications during the transition. The issue related to the question of how mining activities might impact neighbors such as Corkscrew Swamp and a large seed and plant growing operation that depended heavily on a certain level of available water.

The report delicately agreed with all the applicant's points until it came to the issue of groundwater. "If the applicant can demonstrate that the proposed mine will maintain groundwater levels (for those water levels will be restored to a level closer to historic levels), the proposed amendment could be found compatible with maintaining (or improving) groundwater resources. If this is not demonstrated through the current zoning review, the proposed amendment to the future lime rock mining overlay identified on Lee Plan Map 14 should not be adopted." All that despite the fact that Map 14 was no longer in effect.

Sakata Farms

The most immediate problem was with Sakata Farms. The mining pits proposed by Troyer would cover 781 acres and be as much as 110 feet deep. This would reduce the groundwater level which Sakata was accustomed to using for irrigation of their fields and greenhouses, and they objected strongly to approval of the permit.

Sakata had also objected to the rezone in 2009. Although it was supported by the hearing examiner at the time, the company knew it would come back and became actively involved in opposing the abandonment of Map 14, taking its case to court where it lost.

With the court's decision, and in looking at the 2019 rezone there was one last hope: the Florida Department of Transportation (FDOT). Since the only exit from the proposed Troyer mine was onto SR 82, the company argued that its intersection was only 60 feet away and getting in and out of its property with 1,600 loaded dump trucks traveling the road each day was an imminent danger. But the road was scheduled for improvement and widening in the Metropolitan Planning Organization in the 2040 planning horizon so the farm's argument went nowhere.

Displacing the Panther

While Sakata was pursuing its objections, the Conservancy and Florida Wildlife Federation had brought up a second problem: destruction of primary Florida panther habitat. With extensive mining pits, a transportation corridor for the animal would be cut off, but the applicant had promised to restore almost 930 acres into preserved wetlands, allowing the big cats to traverse at the north and south ends of the property, despite the fact that the only road for dump truck access would be SR 82 at the north end. There the animals would either have to cross an active road or through a safe passage created beneath the roadway. The objection was dismissed by a promise to duplicate existing travel corridors at both ends of the property, but few specifics were given.

Corkscrew Swamp Sanctuary

The long-range problem even more of a concern was the impact on Audubon's Corkscrew Swamp Sanctuary. The wetland areas of Troyer Brothers property served as part of the headwaters of the swamp. A hydrologic study had been done showing the rapid drawdown of water at Corkscrew. And Audubon, with its large and active membership, was a force to be reckoned with.[92]

Historically, the swamp had been the largest rookery and nesting site in the United States for the threatened wood stork. Neighboring wetlands with variable hydroperiods serve as forage areas for the birds, and if not suitable they will simply move on to another part of the country. According to Audubon's Brad Cornell, "Our whole sanctuary has been impacted by the loss wetlands all around us which are really important factors in whether we have listed species like wood storks nesting here or not."[93] He continued by saying that development and associated drainage had led to a loss of 82% of wet prairies surrounding the swamp, so important for forage by nesting wood storks.

As more questions arose the Lee County Commission and staff began to stonewall inquiries leaving open the question of why industrial use that would drop the level of groundwater near conservation land paid for by taxpayer's dollars would be permitted.

Troyer Brothers refused to be interviewed. In written comments, the company pointed out that the rezone had been approved by FDEP, the SFWMD and the Corps of Engineers. But missing from the comments was the fact that another federal agency was not on board. It was the U.S. Environmental Protection Agency. In a December 2021 letter issued to FDEP, the EPA cited inadequate analysis of impacts using the current definition of wetlands under federal law. The matter was in federal courts at the time in the *Sackett vs Environmental Protection Agency* that would eventually wind up in the Supreme Court with Justice Samuel Alito constructing an extremely narrow definition to exempt over 50% of the nation's wetlands from federal jurisdiction and regulation.

With the uncertainty as to how the court's ruling would affect southwest Florida, Bert Harris suits became the *mode du jour*. The Bert Harris Private Rights Protection Act, passed in 1995, allowed property owners to sue if they felt that government bodies had deprived them of the full value of their property. It became a cudgel that brought county commissions and others to placate plaintiffs with quick settlements.

Florida Farms Development

Two miles from Wild Blue on the south side of Corkscrew Road is the Florida Farms Development project. Owned by the Lipman and Weisinger families, the largest tomato farmers in the country, a request was submitted and denied in 2013 for a 4,652-acre rock mining permit. The Lee County Hearing Examiner recommended that the rezone be denied due to its inconsistency with Map 14. FFD Land Company sued Lee County with a Bert Harris claim, seeking $39 million in damages. The case was settled in October 2020, and with the Lipman family adding nearly 600 additional acres the project ended up at 5,208 acres with the same number of housing units, 100,000 sq. ft. of commercial space and a facility for agricultural research. Population was estimated to be a little over 11,000 souls with GL Homes being the main builder. The property would run south over existing farmland for almost three miles along Six Ls Farm Road. It would be bordered on the west by Flint Pen Strand and on the east by Corkscrew Swamp Sanctuary.

Lee County, coming out of the 2008–2009 recession, had been reducing impact fees and regulatory requirements at a rapid pace, and as a result FFD felt their plan aligned with both the interests of the owners and county officials so would sail through the permitting process.

The FFD project is still in the initial phase, so little is known about the exact design, but the project reflects an inevitable outcome in southwest Florida: more money could be made by growing rooftops than by plowing furrows in the sand.

Kingston

The problem of water starvation into the Audubon site went on steroids when another new development, Kingston, was approved by the Lee County Commission in June 2022 to settle a Bert Harris lawsuit filed by Corkscrew Grove Limited Partnership in 2011. Just to the east of Troyer Brothers property, the company estimated that the value of its lime rock was $63 million.

The site was over 6,600 acres running from SR 82 south to Corkscrew Road and the development plan was for 10,000 homes, 700,000 sq. ft. of commercial space and a 240-room hotel. Proposed density was 1.5 dwelling units per acre, but the application was to develop 3,336 acres—amounting to density of 3 per acre.

The property bordered the Imperial Marsh Preserve as well as conservation lands and Corkscrew Swamp Sanctuary to the south and was in the Environmental Enhancement and Preservation Communities Overlay (EEPCO), a designated overlay to protect and promulgate flow ways and wildlife corridors in southeastern Lee County by permitting higher density in exchange for the developers enhanced environmental restoration. The Conservancy felt

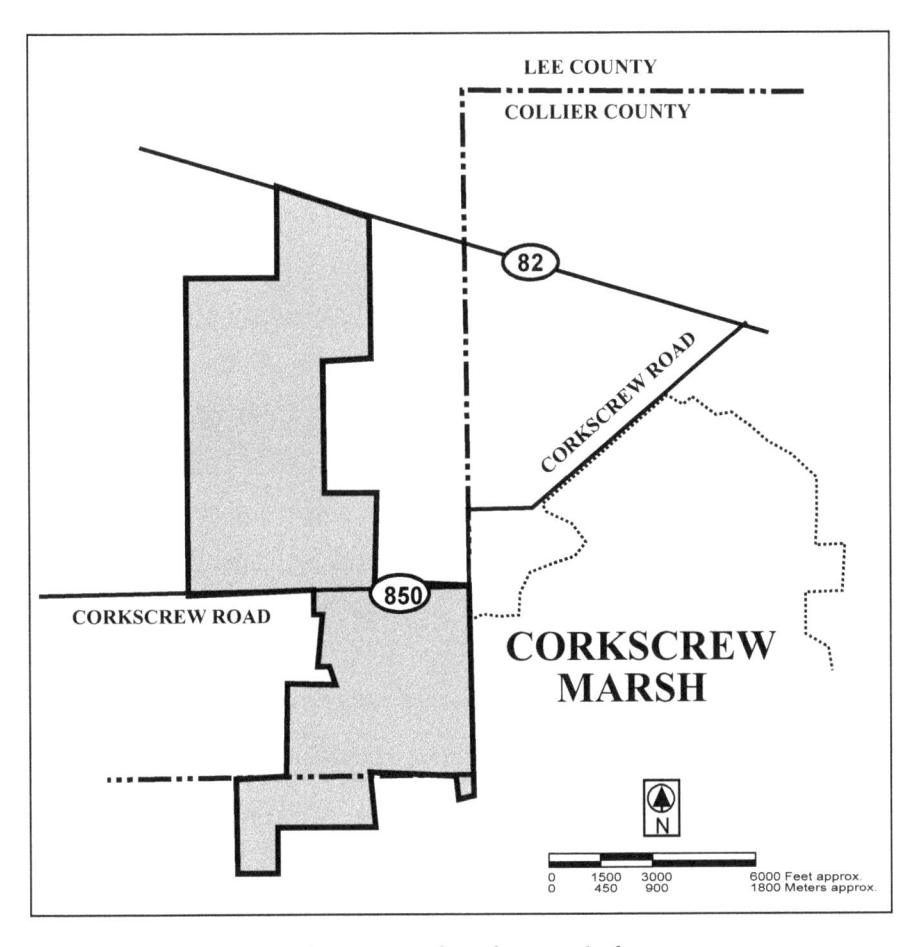

Kingston map by: John G. Beriault

that the project was not aligned with the express purposes of the EEPCO and would have significant negative long-term impacts on the surrounding ecosystem.

Cameratta Companies made the argument that its development would be accompanied by environmental improvements and would be less impactful than either mining or the current level of agricultural operations with its high-water consumption, applications of herbicides and pesticides, and fertilizers. The company promised to finance and build a two-lane access road up the spine of Kingston from Corkscrew Road to SR 82 and said it was working with the local Metropolitan Planning Organization on widening of both arterials. But there was more to it than that because ultimately the Lee County MPO agreed that the new Kingston Ranch Road would be expanded into a four-lane boulevard and incorporated into the 2045 Long Range Transportation Plan (LRTP), taking the cost of expansion and maintenance from the private into the public domain.

The Conservancy's objections focused on a loss of habitat for listed species, the impact of traffic, the cumulative and secondary effects of the project, and finally the lack of suitable alternatives analysis. In a study by Dr. Robert Frakes in 2015, he found that 4,774 acres of the site were considered to be adult panther breeding habitat.[94] When combined with Troyer Mine and FFD, the loss would exceed 7,400 acres. The Conservancy's letter pointed out that the development would generate more than 95,000 vehicle trips per day in an area where panther collisions were high, citing

280 deaths due to encounters with trucks and cars between 1993 and 2022.

A second listed species impacted was the Crested Caracara. The birds had a number of nesting sites on the property and research from the USFWS indicated that mitigation was an option much less desirable than avoidance because of the desire to return to the same nesting habitat.[95] Wood storks were also on the site, once favored but in declining numbers due to the altered hydrology of nearby Corkscrew Swamp Sanctuary and a decrease in forage areas.

The Conservancy also returned to one of the lingering problems plaguing the permitting process in south Florida: the unforeseen cumulative impacts of destroying natural wetlands through dredge and fill with each project being reviewed independent of all others. Going back to the days of litigation over the Mirasol development at the bottom of the CREW, the Conservancy once again addressed the lack of analysis of cumulative and secondary effects. In a letter to the District Director of FDEP in June 2023, the Conservancy warned that "the 404 Handbook requires that FDEP conduct a secondary impact analysis particularly when a proposal that may impact areas like the CREW and Corkscrew Swamp Sanctuary which may be affected by the proposed dredge or fill activities."[96]

Finally the objections centered on a lack of an appropriate alternatives analysis. Believing that there was no public benefit to the project, the Conservancy noted with particular emphasis that Kingston was smack in the middle of the

DR/GR, the major source of water for Lee County. It then cited the list of criteria set forth by the applicant arguing they were so restrictive there was simply no possibility of even considering alternative locations, tantamount to allowing the fox to design the hen house.

And, to leave no stone unturned, in the last paragraph of the letter was this: "Please note that this letter does not constitute support for the state assumed section 404 permitting program, which we believe is unlawful." [97]

Cameratta Companies responded that it had always, in its appearances and testimony before regulatory bodies, promised to build into its developments a series of storm water runoff outfalls, and to use water management techniques that would enhance, rather than reduce, both quality and quantity of water in the region.

The company's chairman was a bit less delicate. "The federal government should stay out of the way. They're not benefitting anybody. They're making us delay and pay more money." [98]

All Together Now

Taken together the two building projects would add 15,000 homes over the next five years and take the population on East Corkscrew to something north of 57,000 souls.

The federal government had, for the most part, gotten "out of the way." With the state in control of 404 permitting, 125 of the pending applications were within a 10-mile radius of Kingston, but there was a larger lesson to be drawn from the deep dive by the Conservancy and its partners, and that was exposing a desire by FDEP to prove that the state could do it faster with a lack of fully trained personnel, and could lead to either a superficial or cursory review as in the deficient alternatives analysis. EPA was still there as a second but unreliable filter. The loss of some federal agency reviews may have made the process more acceptable to Joe Cameratta, but less certain in the Conservancy's view as to the long-term preservation of south Florida's natural resources.

The story now turns to another of the Conservancy's challenges: how Florida became the third state in the country to assume 404 permitting, opening the floodgates to new development with hasty approval as its hallmark. Historically applicants needed to seek both state and federal approval, but in 2017, with a super majority in the legislature and a go-go attitude toward development and total disregard of environmental effects, the administration of Gov. Rick Scott decided to get rid of the Corps and other federal agencies to expedite permitting.

404 Program

Sec. 404 of the Clean Water Act provides that the federal government, through the U.S. Army Corps of Engineers, Environmental Protection Agency, U.S. Fish and Wildlife Service and National Marines Fisheries Service (NMFS) shall review all applications for the discharge of wastewater, including materials from dredge and fill, into the navigable waters of the United States where the Corps had jurisdiction.

In the law was a Section, 404(g)(1), allowing the governor of any state to assume full jurisdiction of permitting. Taking advantage of this, in 2018 with the anti-environmental Rick Scott in the governor's office and a compliant Trump administration in Washington, Florida's legislature passed a bill that gave the Florida Department of Environmental Protection authority to begin the process of public rulemaking to assume control of 404 permits. According to the state's website, the intent was to "better protect the state's wetlands and surface waters by assuming the federal dredge and fill permitting program under section 404 of the federal Clean Water Act within certain waters."[99]

The rulemaking process was complicated but hastily completed on July 21, 2020, to allow enough time for review and comment in order to beat the January 21, 2021, deadline when the Trump administration would leave office. The relevant documents were a Memorandum of Understanding between FDEP and the Corps to address issues of procedure and authority and a second between the Florida Fish and Wildlife Conservation Commission (FWC) and the USFWS proposing a coordinated "consultation" on threatened and endangered species coordination, with the USFWS retaining responsibility for Habitat Conservation Plans. EPA would retain general oversight of permits being issued by the state.

Through this process a "State 404 Program," was being created to satisfy the requirements of federal law not already addressed by Florida's existing Environmental Resource Permitting (ERP) program.[100] Minor changes were made to the ERP rules to ease matters along.[101] Florida submitted its package to the EPA on Aug. 20, 2020. The next step was public comment.

The state program would be responsible for overseeing permitting for any project proposing dredge and fill activities within state "assumed waters." Such projects included, but were not limited to: single family residences; commercial developments; utility projects; environmental restoration and enhancement; linear transportation projects; governmental development; certain agricultural and silvicultural activities; and in-water work within freshwater bodies such as boat ramps, living shorelines and other shoreline stabilization.

Supported heavily by developers and miners, and known quietly as the "Holy Grail," FDEP trumpeted that assumption of 404 permitting would provide a streamlined procedure within which both federal and state requirements would be fully addressed. It would provide greater certainty to the regulated community, speeding up the approval process for both the applicant and agencies, and afford the state greater control over its natural resources while complying with federal law. Projects within state-assumed waters would require both an ERP and state 404 authorization but filing for the latter was intended to remain separate from the existing ERP program.

The heart of the argument was that the process would be more efficient since approximately 85% of review requirements overlapped between the ERP and 404 applications, eliminating duplicative review. Based on that, FDEP said no more money would be required to administer review of both.

Objections by Earthjustice and the Conservancy

The Conservancy was convinced that in attempting to bulldoze the change through before the Trump administration departed, both federal and state agencies overran the necessary due diligence, and a consortium of environmental groups, led by a lawyer from Earthjustice, tried to call time out.

But the state was smart. In an attempt to divide environmental communities in Florida, it had already locked up support from the Everglades Foundation with its wealthy and influential board of directors, many of whom were supporters of Gov. Ron DeSantis.

On September 4, 2020, EPA announced that it had received "a complete program submission" from the State of Florida as the first step to taking over 404 permitting.

It brought an immediate response from Sierra Club, backed by the Conservancy and Center for Biological Diversity, claiming that a Collier County Eastern Lands HCP had been deferred to a later date to await takeover of 404 permitting by the state. The three organizations questioned whether acreage promised to be set aside in the HCP would actually be put into a category of permanent conservation. They felt that contiguity of lands for habitat and animal corridors had to be part of an iron-clad written commitment on the part of the landowners seeking approval for the plan, and that monitoring and enforcement provisions were seriously lacking in the proposal. The Sierra Club letter said "...the proposed HCP left these critically important determinations to be made piecemeal during the CWA 404 permitting process for each project, evidently by FWS during the associated Section 7 ESA consultation process for 404 permits."[102] In other words, cumulative effects would be ignored by taking individual applications on a one-by-one basis without looking at the eastern lands as a whole.

The whole process was also purposefully truncated because "...the Florida Department of Environmental Protection ... has made clear its intent that the ... EPA conduct a *one-time ESA 7 (a) (2) consultation regarding Florida FDEP's assumption of 404 permitting authority and that it believes no further consultations with the services will be required thereafter.*" [Italics by author] [103]

What was concerning was that as part of the deal FDEP had assured the Eastern Collier Property Owners Association (ECPO) that when it took over 404 permitting the review would be restricted and limited to checking compliance with the HCP and then seeking concurrence from FWS. [104] But, argued Sierra, the plan had absolutely no mechanism, i.e., monitoring and enforcement, to ensure that contiguous habitat and promised corridors would be included as development occurred.

An even larger problem loomed. By having the state take over wetlands permitting the National Environmental Policy Act (NEPA) would not apply. Passed in the 1970s it was a powerful law creating the Council on Environmental Quality. It was designed to allow citizens to question development in critical lands and to insist upon an Environmental Impact Statement (EIS). With no EIS a lot problems could be swept away by simply being ignored.

The Conservancy's Amber Crooks, Environmental Policy Manager, agrees. "There is no substitute for NEPA. The state's Environmental Impact Statement does not have any of the important protective measures like the Endangered Species Act, coastal protection, and the federal cultural and historic preservation laws..." [105]

The Sierra Club objections were followed by an October 23, 2020, letter from Earthjustice. It looked at the whole issue of permitting from a different perspective and claimed that the submission was in fact incomplete, preventing meaningful public comment. Objections came in three parts.

First, echoing Sierra Club's point, the application did not specify how the state would offer adequate protection to listed species as required by the no-jeopardy provision in the law. The state in its application had indicated it was negotiating with the USFWS and NMFS but the results of those discussions had not been included in the submittal document.

The ESA required that federal agencies consult with the USFWS before they approved any project that might affect either listed species or critical habitat. The process normally begins with an informal consultation, then advances to a more structured presentation if the action proposed will likely adversely affect a listed species. The appropriate agency, USFWS, or in the case of species under jurisdiction of the NMFS, must then issue a "biological opinion" analyzing the effects of the proposal on habitat and species.

If the project jeopardizes the "continued existence of a listed species or destroys or adversely modifies designated critical habitat," either Service will issue a "jeopardy opinion" requiring alternatives or modifications to advance the project. A second part of the opinion is an incidental take statement exempting certain effects on listed species from provisions of the law requiring an estimate of the number of individuals likely to be taken or the extent of protected habitat that might be either disturbed or destroyed.

One of the species of greatest concern for the Conservancy was the iconic Florida panther, the state mammal. The ESA required a review of the panther population be done every five years but the most recent had been issued in 2009, and Crooks believed that before any projects were approved by the state that an updated review was necessary. Her fear was that with the flood of applications, decisions would be made absent relevant and timely information about the status of the big cat's range and population.

By moving the process to a "technical assistance consultation" between the state and the two federal wildlife agencies involved, the terms of the ESA would no longer apply. The agencies involved in moving 404 permitting to Florida developed a questionable method by which incidental takes from activities during and after the development was completed would be contemplated after the take coverage was already granted through the state's blank check programmatic "biological opinion." Here again, the Conservancy was concerned that the state's seizure of permitting was inconsistent with the letter of the law and monitoring and reporting would be largely ignored, resulting in less protection for listed species like the panther.

Second, argued Earthjustice, the state's application failed to clearly distinguish between "assumed waters" and "retained waters." It was an important distinction.

The "assumed waters" were rather simply defined as those not retained by the Corps of Engineers under the Rivers and Harbors Act of 1899. The "retained waters" were in an appendix dated August 23, 2019, part of an earlier attempt by the state to take over the 404 permitting.

During the earlier 2017-2019 attempt, the Corps had issued a notice terminating the comment period after three weeks saying it would be reopened upon "further notice." That never happened. Earthjustice made the point forcefully that the 2019 list of federal "retained waters" was only four pages whereas the earlier 2017 list was seventeen pages long.

Finally, Earthjustice argued that the state's application was seriously deficient in describing the steps it would take to fully implement, review and monitor the program. FDEP was already straining to meet its existing obligations. Its budget had been hit hard by the Scott administration in 2014 during a stampede to reduce regulations. The new application was submitted in the midst of the COVID-19 pandemic when state revenues were seriously affected and the DeSantis administration had asked all departments to cut 8.5% out of their budgets for 2021.

The conclusion of the filing was a blunt verbal cudgel. "The department's claim that it will be able to operate a Section 404 program without any additional funding from the state—a fundamentally flawed premise that the legislature relied on when granting the authority for the state agency to pursue assumption—is untenable. It either reflects the departments erroneous belief that Section

404 is merely "duplicative" of state regulations (it is not), demonstrates the department's intention to treat its pre-existing regulations and Section 404 as one and the same (it may not), or suggests that the department simply will not adequately implement, operate or enforce a Section 404 program (it cannot)." [106]

The objection letter concluded with a request to extend the comment period until the state cured gaps in the application and resubmitted it as a truly complete and finished document.

The request was ignored and EPA approved Florida's program on Dec. 17, 2020, to become effective on Dec. 22, 2020." [107] The only redeeming feature was the fact that the program would still have some advisory oversight by EPA.

The Conservancy was late to the party but its position was clear: "FDEP moved forward to assume the program despite a massive budget shortfall, stating that they could take on the federal program with no additional funding." [108] Its interest in maintaining federal review and control of the 404 permitting processes harkened back to 2005 when the Corps denied a permit for the Mirasol development along Immokalee Road. The decision was based upon the inadequacy of a drainage ditch that would dramatically affect water outflow from Audubon's Corkscrew Swamp Sanctuary. But at the same time the Corps had issued a permit for another development adjacent to Mirasol called Parklands, where the developer, Ronto Development

Parklands Inc., had quickly sent in the bulldozers to begin filling in wetlands.

Mirasol altered its development plans a number of times over the next two years and finally received a permit from the Corps in 2007 immediately challenged in court by the National Wildlife Federation on behalf of a group called the Cocohatchee Coalition of which the Conservancy was a founding member. In 2009 a federal judge in Miami ruled that the Corps had violated the Administrative Procedures Act (APA) and NEPA by not looking at the cumulative impacts of nearby developments. The court also ruled that the USFWS violated the APA and ESA by issuing a favorable biological opinion. This forced Mirasol to change its application resulting in a decrease in housing units and a widening of the water control outflow canal enhancing drainage from Corkscrew. The Conservancy's thinking was this case stood out as a shining example of the value of having multiple agencies, both state and federal, involved in the permitting process.

Another case on point in the pipeline from an earlier time was an HCP submitted by ECPO and its members in 2009. Covering approximately 45,000 acres of the eastern lands, it was supported by Audubon Florida, Florida Wildlife, Federation, Defenders of Wildlife, and Audubon of the Western Everglades but the Conservancy had its own objections. Nicole Johnson reflected on this. "I think this was pivotal moment in the organization's history—when we walked away. Of all the environmental groups involved not having the Conservancy was a real blow."

As the real estate market began to pick up, ECPO resubmitted its request for a multi-species HCP for the eastern lands. Then, in July 2022, the landowners pulled the application. For the HCP to be approved an incidental take statement had to be issued and there was the possibility that a jeopardy opinion was forthcoming from the USFWS. Using the Freedom of Information Act the Conservancy obtained a number of documents relating to the application causing Crooks to comment "it is pretty clear to us that the impact from the HCP would not have been authorized. The problem was traffic; once we knew it was the traffic that the USFWS cared the most about, we definitely keyed in on that. They were hung up on traffic. The mortality rate from roadkill would increase significantly and perhaps jeopardize the future of the animal."[109] The ECPO withdrawal allowed it to move the approval process to the state to avoid the embarrassment of a possible federal jeopardy opinion and join the parade of developers eager for approval of their pet projects.

FDEP "Fesses Up"

In its second annual report, FDEP noted that over 6,000 applications had flooded the department and that 2,280 had been withdrawn for either inadequacies or concerns expressed during review. By June 30, 2022, the agency had issued 296 permits and denied 90 (most of which would come back with slight modifications). In its self-congratulatory summary, the department noted that Florida's Sunshine Laws made information more readily available than when the Corps was issuing permits, and that the state's ERP regulations assured there would be no net loss of wetlands. However, that could be accomplished by using mitigation banks far from the site of wetlands destruction. Florida was good at finding ways that avoidance could be ignored by making other alternatives available, but that was about to go too.

The report chimed in that the ERP program protected isolated wetlands better than the federal 404 which related to navigable waters. However, on almost the same page boasted that "Florida utilizes several rapid assessment methods to determine the loss and gain of wetland functions. Rapid assessment methods are more appropriate than ratio methods because they use ecological principles to calculate functional loss and gain units rather than simply quantitative descriptions and acreages." [110] In plain language, what this meant was that wetlands' acreage lost in a development would not be replaced on a one-for-one basis anywhere else in the state, but that a misty qualitative judgment on "function" would be made as to how many mitigated acres would be the equivalent of those lost. This was aligned with the state's long-standing preference to avoid hard numbers.

Florida was remarkably consistent in its multiple attempts to hasten permitting resulting in wetlands destruction, harkening back to the Harvey Harper methodology enshrined in 2003. Harper was a consultant hired by a group called Water Enhancement and Restoration Coalition backed by Bonita Bay Group, a powerful developer in Lee and Collier County. He built a model and looking at the results concluded that wetlands contributed to downstream pollution because nutrients at the outlet were higher than at the input point, and therefore all wetlands polluted at a single uniform rate, adjusted for detention time, regardless of location and that constructed wet detention ponds were more reliable. Harper's work was peer-reviewed in 2005 by Versar Inc. a Virginia company and later by the Center for Watershed Protection, in Maryland, hired by the Conservancy despite the fact that Harper had tweaked the model in 2007.[111] Nothing ever came of either review because the state at the time, according to FDEP Secretary Mike Sole, was interested only in "streamlining" the process.

While all this was going on a case before the U.S. Supreme Court was about to dramatically change the definition of the boundaries of a wetland.

The Sackett Case

The 1972 Clean Water Act made it illegal to fill, drain, or pollute the "waters of the United States" without a permit from the federal government and in some cases from state regulators.

However, the Pacific Legal Foundation, working on behalf of Michael and Chantel Sackett, brought a case that ended up in United States Supreme Court. [112] The topic was whether or not the protections in effect at the time covered all wetlands, both continuously flowing and seasonal. Developers and miners had argued for years that the broad application of the law was overly restrictive and denied them their rights as property owners. When the *Sackett v. Environmental Protection Agency* decision was announced Justice Alito wrote, on behalf of 5-4 majority, that the law applied only to wetlands known to have a "continuous surface connection" to another larger water body. Alito's opinion was similar to another case brought in 2006, *Rapanos v. United States*, in which the test was equally narrowly defined.

The Sackett's were property owners of a ½ acre plot in Idaho's Panhandle adjacent to Priest Lake. After filling a part of their lot with gravel they were fined for noncompliance of EPA regulations. They had never attempted to obtain a permit and walked away from the property in 2007. The Pacific Legal Foundation argued that the wetlands filled in were not "navigable waters," and that law did not apply. The court agreed but then expanded by applying it to seasonal wetlands throughout the country, covering as much as 51% of all identified and regulated wetlands. In the American west, where the Sackett's had the property, over 94% of pond-like wetlands (under the broadest definition) are intermittently moist, and the court's decision removed temporary streams such as those that result from either snowmelt or wet season rains that ultimately feed into larger water bodies.

The definition of "navigable waters" over which the Corps had unquestioned jurisdiction had been bounced back and forth between Democratic and Republican administrations for years, with the Trump appointed EPA cutting back on Pres. Obama's definitions. That was later changed back by Pres. Biden's EPA. The variety of interpretations was based upon application of a series of conflicting decisions in which courts said the term applied to waters with a "significant nexus" to a fully navigable waterway.

But Alito went on to explain that the way to measure a true wetland was only if it was not difficult to determine where the wetland ended and the receiving water body began. If the connection was either tenuous or seasonal then the Clean Water Act would not apply. The ruling was overly broad in that it appeared to apply to only surface waters and not to any connections existing below the immediate layer of topsoil, but by using the word "difficult" it allowed interpretation to vary depending upon who was calling the shots.

Florida Calls the Shots

In the eight years from 2012–2020 the Corps had control over wetlands permitting it received 8,699 applications and denied one. While Florida's second annual report through 2022 showed a little over 6,000 applications, new March 2023 data showed, in the little over two years since 404 permitting was taken over, it received 6,405 applications and turned down 145—most for amendments and corrections. The pace was torrid and unrelenting. Mining and development companies throughout the state were delighted; the "Holy Grail" was finally in the right hands.

The Coast and the Corps

Florida's vulnerability to hurricanes—on both coasts—is legendary. Since 1851 Collier County has been hit by thirty-three storms, twenty at Category 3 or higher. The numeric system, from Category 1 to 5 is based on the Saffir-Simpson wind scale ranking a hurricane's maximum sustained wind speed. It also helps to estimate property damage, but does not consider storm surge. To measure that locally, a tidal gauge was placed at Naples Bay by the National Oceanic and Atmospheric Administration (NOAA) in 1965 to quantify peak surge. The average was about 2 feet until Hurricane Irma in 2017, which topped out at 4.62 feet (adjusted for tidal changes).

Irma was the most powerful storm ever recorded in the open Atlantic Ocean. It became a Category 5 on September 5th and tore into the Florida Keys, Miami, and Broward County with sustained winds of over 130 miles-per-hour. It caused 83 deaths, ruptured and flooded over 65,000 structures and cost nearly $50 billion, over double the $20-$25 billion cost of Hurricane Andrew in 1992.

Crossing the state, it hit Collier County destroying over 1,000 homes, causing property damage of over $300 million and two deaths. Sustained winds were over 100 miles-per-hour with the strongest recorded gust 142 mph at Naples Airport.

The storm prompted the City of Miami and Miami-Dade County to engage the U.S. Army Corps of Engineers to do a study of hardening the coastline to protect what was estimated at the time to be $40 billion worth of coastal and inland property assets. Miami had been experiencing king tides for years, described as "... a higher-than-normal tide typically lasting about 3 hours occurring annually and predictably in September through November. King tides may cause residents to experience 'sunny day flooding' where a street or other areas will temporarily become flooded when it is not raining."[113]

The Corps unveiled its Miami plan in 2020. By creating a series of floodgates across rivers and a 1-mile floodwall along the waterfront, and a 30-foot-high wall in part of Biscayne Bay, the estimated cost was $4.6 billion. Land acquisition was a little over $400 million but the Corps admitted the project would only reduce storm surge damage and not have any impact on king tides. The design was preliminary and intended to elicit public comment which was immediate and generally negative. A Miami City Commissioner, Ken Russell, put it succinctly: "The $40 billion in assets you are trying to protect will be diminished if you build a wall around downtown because you're going to affect market values and quality of life."[114]

The Collier County Commission, after surveying the damage from Irma, took the same approach as Miami by engaging the Corps to do an environmental impact statement and cost-benefit analysis for a Coastal Storm Risk Management (CSRM) feasibility study. A draft copy was released in 2020. The Tentatively Selected Plan (TSP) would include beach berm and dune[115] renourishment of approximately 9.5 miles along the Gulfcoast: "...two surge barriers with sector gates across Wiggins Pass and Doctors Pass, two jetties at Wiggins Pass, concrete structures in the dune system adjacent to Wiggins Pass, a Bonita Beach Road floodwall and surge barrier, Seagate Drive floodwall and sluice gate, Tamiami Trail floodwall and surge barrier, and associated pump stations, currently tentatively located at Wiggins Pass, Doctors Pass, and the Tamiami Trail."[116] (These will each be dealt with in detail later). Height of the beach dunes was expected to be between 12 and 14 feet, the berm would range from 50 to 150 feet wide and floodwalls from 10 to 14 feet. The last point in the TSP included artificial reef structures near Marco Island to dissipate storm surge.

Ian

Irma was bad enough but then in 2022, Hurricane Ian became the deadliest ever to hit the State of Florida. Making its way up the Gulf of Mexico it moved into the west coast after decimating western Cuba, packing winds of 160 mph and made landfall on Cayo Costa Island in Lee County. The damage to Sanibel Island and Cape Coral was mainly from wind, and the impact on Naples and Collier County primarily from storm surge of 8 to 10 feet. Water continued to move inland and combined with tropical rainfall, covered US 41 with as much as 6 feet of surge as far east as Carnestown. The flood trapped people in their houses and decimated one fire station as well as a hospital emergency bay in North Naples. The cost to the City of Naples was estimated at $989 million, $255 million in Marco Island and $7 million in Everglades City. Ian damaged over 3,500 structures with a total loss in the county estimated at $2.2 billion.

The devastation forced the County Commission to ask the Corps to reopen the 2020 CSRM plan and hold public hearings to move the process forward. In doing so the county became the local sponsoring partner responsible for 35% of the cost of the ultimate plan.

Modeling of the earlier TSP was based upon six segments, beginning with Planning Area 1 which ran from Bonita Beach Road along the coast down to Vanderbilt Beach Road. A floodwall would start at the coast and run along Bonita Beach Road. It would be almost 6,000 feet with floodgates designed to remain open to permit traffic to flow until a hurricane approached when they would be closed. The floodwall would be 12 feet high. At Wiggins Pass, floodwalls would be built into the dune and berm system along the coast with mechanical gates attached serving as a surge barrier anchored by two jetties projecting out into the Gulf.

Planning Area 2 would cover the area from Vanderbilt Beach Road south to Seagate. A dune and berm system would run down the coast and Clam Pass would remain open as the single tidal inlet.

In Planning Area 3 an east-west seawall would be built out to Gulf Shore Boulevard, approximately 4,500 feet long with one sluice gate leading from South Clam Pass Bay into Venetian Bay. A surge barrier would be located at Doctors Pass anchored by two hardened floodwalls on either side built into the dune and berm system.

Planning Area 4 was the most complicated. Running down along the coast to Gordon Pass would be the standard nature-based dune and berm barrier. A floodwall would be built from Central Avenue in the City of Naples down US 41, turning east and crossing the Gordon River where a surge barrier and sluice gate would be located to allow the Gordon River to flow into Naples Bay. The floodwall would continue down on US 41 to Court House Shadows at Palm Drive. A possible pump station was also located just below Tin City.

The Conservancy found this unworkable. In a white paper by Kathy Worley and April Olson, they pointed out: "As an example, if the US 41 floodwall were to be built and gates were closed bay front and rear park communities have the potential to become flooded due to impoundment of storm water after torrential hurricane rains."[117] And, if the gates were closed along the floodwall, it would block water from moving up Naples Bay, into the Gordon River, and into bordering riparian areas to moderate the surge and spread the water out for percolation.

Planning Area 6 was Marco Island where a berm and dune system would be constructed along the coast down to the hardened and existing revetment area bordering the Gulf entrance to Caxambas above Allan Key.

The Conservancy Takes the Lead

Nicole Johnson and April Olson believed that the 2020 TSP had three glaring weaknesses: the first was that it focused on inbound surge only; second, the use of natural ecosystems was ignored; and third, the analysis failed to take into account the cost-benefit of natural (as opposed to structural) solutions.

In more detail, to the first point the study ignored the effects of inland flooding from rainwater and storm water runoff. Some hurricanes, depending upon speed, could dump as much as 20 inches of rain. When impounded, with the proposed sluice gates and floodgates all closed, inland storm water loaded with nutrients and other forms of urban pollution could impact ground water and the surface aquifers a number of exurban residents use as their source of drinking water. By sequestering urban runoff behind the closed gates, the nutrient laden water would increase the potential for algal blooms and serve as a stimulus to red tide once the floodgates were opened and water released. Beyond trapping inland water, they were concerned with "seaward flooding, storm surge stacking and wave displacement seaward of the walls and gates (flow around the gates)."[118]

Their second and third objections were interrelated and as an alternative, the Conservancy policy experts recommended the Corps look at a Multiple Line of Defense Strategy (MLDS), something the Corps was intimately familiar with through its Network-Engineering with Nature (N–EWM) program. Among its partners were the University of Florida Center for Coastal Solutions, The Nature Conservancy and Stantec, the company responsible for the complicated credit program adopted for the eastern lands of Collier County.

MLDS used a series of constructed and natural measures to mitigate coastal flooding beginning offshore with breakwater groins, then moving toward the shore with oyster and coral reefs, mangrove forests, and finally beach and dune restoration for shoreline stabilization.

One notable example of stabilization was a restoration project on Virginia Key in Monroe County. Beginning in 2013 the Ocean Foundation, working with the city and volunteers, planted 37,000 plugs, mainly native sea oats, along the coast. Sea oats have long roots that push deep into the dunes and when Hurricane Irma blew through in 2017 the dunes trapped new sand, increasing in size and protecting inland areas, providing an example of how beachfront plants could adapt to the forces of nature and use wave action to enhance protection of inland properties.

The Cost-Benefit Analysis

An example of nature-based solutions was an analysis done by the Nature Conservancy in 2019 studying the effect of mangroves on the financial impact of losses after hurricane Irma. The stated purpose of the study was "... to understand where and how the physical effects of mangroves on extreme water levels translate to risk reduction benefits to people, property and infrastructure.... There has been little large-scale quantitative analysis of the economic contribution mangroves make on flooding impacts. But industries with high interest in coastal property, such as insurance or real estate development, need this information to price in the effect of mangroves on flood risk. We aim to fill this knowledge gap by using a catastrophe modeling approach to quantitatively estimate the economic impacts of mangroves on flood damages to coastal properties in Florida."[119]

Using standard World Bank methodology to estimate risk reduction benefits, the authors modeled 100 different possible storm events to create a series of probabilities for Collier County. They then took actual data from Hurricane Irma using multiple parameters including forward speed, air pressure, and water levels to compare the actual flood footprint with modeled recalculation after all coastal mangroves were converted to open waters, computing calculated savings to property at 25.5%.

The study concluded that "mangrove forest belts act as barriers or baffles, increasing surge water levels immediately seaward of the belt and decreasing water levels behind it. In Collier County, development on the seaward side of mangroves experienced an increase in flooding."[120]

The Conservancy's third point about natural ecosystems not being included in the cost-benefit analysis was a big bite. Army Corps policy requires plans to provide positive economic benefits, but the TSP put forth in 2020 failed to account for the economic benefits of natural infrastructure. It also acknowledged negative impacts on a number of endangered or threatened species that would affect the commercial and sport fishing industries, both major segments of southwest Florida's economy.

According to the Corps' own earlier CSRM "Collier County's commercial fisheries are of significant value to the local economy; the number of people employed by the Marine economy generally ranges from nearly 17,000 to 26,000, which comprises between 12% and 18% of total employment in Collier County."[121] Despite that comment, there was little assessment of the negative impact on that industry.

A second impact of hardened structures would be the effect on beaches used by tourists, turtles and birds. Collier County beaches are all regularly renourished. They vary from 30 feet to 100 feet wide and the pounding of wash along and against floodwalls and barriers would erode the sand more quickly than surge on existing beaches.

A white paper by Kathy Worley and April Olson cited the importance of tourism: "As an example, 773,529 people visit

Delnor-Wiggins Pass State Park annually which provides a $92.8 million economic impact and supports 1,300 local jobs."[122] Walls would reduce beach areas for recreation and create an ugly backdrop.

The Conservancy argued that the impact on listed species would be equally disruptive. Three sea turtle species use Collier County beaches for nesting, and are all very particular. When they return to their natal beaches, before building nests they test the quality of the sand and even though their geolocation system tells them they are in the right spot, if the granularity of the beach sand is different from their recollection, they will not nest.

Sea turtles tend to build their nests above the mean high tide line to prevent overwash. The large loggerheads, critically endangered under the federal Endangered Species Act and by statute in Florida's Marine Turtle Protection Act, will lay their eggs closer to the water when encountering hardened structures. Loggerhead turtles nest from Big Hickory Pass in Lee County down to Doctors Pass and then from Gordon Pass along the coast and on barrier islands like Keeywadin down to Big Marco Pass, a total of nearly 30 miles. Inundation of the nests during high tide and even minor storm events becomes possible reducing the birthrate.

Green sea turtles, another endangered species, tend to nest closer to where the coastal dunes are stabilized with vegetation such as sea oats. Finally, the leatherback rarely nests on Collier County beaches but would have to be regarded in the Corps' analysis.

A number of endangered birds and threatened birds use beaches primarily for forage. With hardened structures and rapidly eroding sand the environment for various invertebrates that form a major part of that food chain would be severely compromised.

The Corps eventually backed off all coastal hardening projects except the flood gates at Wiggins Pass. The most severe, the one running down US 41 to Palm Drive, was the first to go as the Corps felt public sentiment was moving strongly toward nature-based solutions.

A Multi-county Strategy

Another glaring error of the Collier 2020 TSP was the fact that it, much like the Miami project, was conceived in isolation from adjacent counties such as Lee to the north and Monroe to the south. Had Regional Planning Councils, virtually eliminated by Gov. Rick Scott, still been effective and functioning entities, they might have stepped up as willing partners, taking the studies beyond county lines.

In the alternative, the State of Florida could have taken responsibility for an overall plan for its coasts but once again the destruction of the entire statewide planning process prevented this from happening when Gov. Scott closed the Department of Community Affairs. With over 8,000 miles of shoreline, it would make sense to employ economies of scale available on a statewide basis, and thereby offer some relief to poorer counties whose budgets would be severely stressed by having to contribute 35% of the cost of protecting their coastlines.

One Final Stinky Problem

There is one more issue not yet discussed in either the 2020 TSP or in 2023 conversations between the Corps, county and the public. That is the problem of old septic tanks. With water impoundment behind a series of seawalls, combined with heavy rainfall during storms, it's likely that elevation of the water table will exceed the bottom of a number of septic tank drain fields.

The original standard statewide for tanks required the bottom be six inches above the water table. Today it is now two feet between the drain field and high-water level during wet season. A septic tank depends heavily on bacteria at the lower levels to break down waste and spread it in the drain field. Each tank was sized for a certain number of people in the house, but in many older neighborhoods there is now more crowding forcing the septic system to function above its rated capacity. In addition, as density increases in developed areas, the soil is simply unable to handle the level of contaminants being soaked up by the aquifers and nearby waterways. The result, obvious recently, has been increased algal blooms like red tide and the killing of sea grasses, a dietary staple of the Florida manatee.

About seventeen pounds of nitrogen waste is produced by one person each year. As it moves outward through the drain field, if the soil is dry it will partially evaporate, but if it is wet will be forced into the groundwater system with trace organics, medications and other human ingested effluents.

Collier County has over 45,000 septic tanks, Monroe County over 25,000. Lee County with 133,000 is the second highest in the state after Miami-Dade. Overall, in Florida there are approximately 2.7 million septic tanks mostly along rivers and coastal areas where people have settled. The State of Florida has danced around this topic for years. The state legislature in 2008 required regular inspections of older tanks but the replacement cost, about $20,000, or the hookup cost to municipal systems at about $5,000 each, would stress older homeowners on fixed incomes and two years later the legislature backed off.

In south Florida water flows to the southwest, so what has origins in Lee County ends up in Collier. If seawalls were to be built, nitrogen laden groundwater would back up against the structures with the inevitable result.

Nature-based Solutions

The Conservancy's white paper wrapped it up this way: "Natural infrastructure is often less expensive than engineered solutions, and may even be free of costs. Nature not only provides protection from wind, waves, erosion, flooding, and storms, but is important for maintaining water quality, providing habitats, and for providing abundant recreational opportunities." In essence the Conservancy was seeking a more holistic solution.

The concept of nature-based solutions was not new to the Corps. In 2021 a directive was issued saying that future analyses "... must evaluate and provide a complete accounting, consideration and documentation of the total benefits of alternative plans across all benefit categories. Total benefits include a summation of monetized and/or quantified benefits, along with a complete accounting of qualitative benefits, for project alternatives across national and regional economic, environmental and social benefit categories." [123]

The language emphasized the importance of regional environmental benefits beyond the self-imposed geographic boundaries of the CSRM into Lee and Monroe counties. It would require including ecosystem elements, many to be embodied in recommendations from the N-EWM group within the Corps as opposed to engineering solutions only.

The Conservancy's leadership at that moment in time was critical. Public meetings included large groups and opinions aired with little central focus. Final outcome was an extension of the deadline to recommend new alternatives, or to modify the 2020 CSRM, with the next draft due in June 2025, giving the public, businesses, county staff and citizens time to study best practices of similar projects throughout the world. It would also allow regional coordination and cooperation to coalesce, a critical aspect in future solutions.

Rob Moher's take on it was straightforward. "I think that without the leadership of the Conservancy, some of the most impractical ideas in the original plan might have gone to the next step. We were instrumental in slowing the process down, and that was the right thing to do. It gives us time to look at nature-based options."[124]

Kathy Worley expanded on his point. "In one of the last meetings, a member of the Corps team told me that they had done similar studies in New York and Miami, but neither compared to the level of public engagement in Collier County, attributable to organizing efforts of the Conservancy."[125]

Care for Sick and Injured Wildlife

Today's von Arx Wildlife Hospital is a well-staffed and amply funded operation integral to the Conservancy's mission to preserve land, water and wildlife. But it was never quite so.

In 1971, Bill Merrihue took over as head of the Conservancy's board. He had taken a similar position at Collier County Audubon and grown the membership quickly into what was the third largest local chapter in America. Merrihue knew that the Conservancy, as successful as it had been during the prior seven years, was still limited in space and community support and he wanted to broaden both. His idea was to combine with the Big Cypress Nature Center, located on a small plot of land just to the north of Jungle Larry's, now the Naples Zoo. Its director was Gary Schmelz, and the main thrust of its effort was environmental education in Collier County schools.

In the center's facility was a small area set aside, run by Audubon and staffed by middle and high school students, to take in birds, small mammals and a few turtles that had been injured. It first opened in 1975, licensed by the Florida Game and Freshwater Fish Commission, and became quickly overwhelmed in its first year with more than 100 patients. Merrihue always thought that the care of sick and injured wildlife was a government function and belonged to either the City or the County. Besides some of the mammals had rabies so he was concerned about the possible liability of having young students exposed to those animals. Schmelz, on the other hand, considered the wildlife operation as a small but important adjunct to the main work of the center, because it involved giving high-school students hands-on experience, supplemented with classroom work, in environmental issues.

Another reason Schmelz and Merrihue saw the future of animal rescue differently was because the center's facility was utterly inadequate—being Julius Fleischmann's old beach house which had been trucked to the Golden Gate Boulevard location where it was reassembled. After a great deal of back and forth with Schmelz, Merrihue eventually relented as he saw the educational aspect of the wildlife program and believed he could raise money to support it.

The money would come quickly. Merrihue wanted to build classrooms and an auditorium as a gathering place but the property was landlocked and did not have direct access to a main arterial. He solved the problem by getting the executor of the Fleischmann estate to sell 13.8 acres to the Conservancy with frontage along the headwaters of the Gordon River to allow boat tours along the mangrove-fringed waterway and out into Naples Bay. The deal closed in 1978 and when fundraising began, Merrihue soon realized that a number of major contributors were very supportive of wildlife treatment and rehabilitation.

A new treatment center in a new building was located on the northeast corner of the campus along with a number of flight cages, an entire water and sewer system for residential birds and animals, and a swimming pool for aquatic-related species. A full-time director, Julie Wasserman, was hired and a college intern program was initiated to help with staffing. She increased the hours of operation and installed a separate telephone system to take calls to give advice on how to handle injured animals and birds but the facility was soon once again overrun as word of mouth about the treatment center spread. And as more people moved into Naples, fishing at the Naples Pier became a major source of injuries where a number of birds, primarily pelicans and gulls, were being brought in on practically a daily basis with treble hooks in their beaks and gullets.

In 1992 Joanna Fitzgerald became one of the interns. She had been educated in Wisconsin, served an internship in England in education, and worked at the Brookfield Zoo. Then, in 1994 when a second full-time position opened at the Conservancy's wildlife center, she took it. When asked why she would move to Florida into an overcrowded and inadequate facility she replied: "I knew my life's work would be with animals. I love them, but I also love to educate people and believe the two could be intimately related."

Appointed as director 18 years ago, Fitzgerald is a confident and fast-talking woman. She described her early years at the Conservancy. "You know, that whole old building was overstuffed. There were times we had to put animals in the bathrooms and sinks; we simply had no place to put them. I think we were serving 2,000 and 3,000 hawks and pelicans and gulls and turtles and possums and raccoons and all other kinds of creatures as best we could. But we made it work. I think the amazing thing is we didn't realize how bad it was until we moved into the new von Arx Wildlife Hospital. I can remember that our x-ray machine was in another building and we would have to run over, take pictures, and come back with the animal again if the images were adequate to do it again. There is just no way to describe the difference. Now, we have diagnosis, treatment and rehabilitation in the same place in a modern facility. Today we're able to easily create isolation when it's needed. The quality of care is just so much better."

The von Arx hospital was opened in 2012. It's now staffed by 4 to 5 full-time employees and anywhere from 12 to 15 volunteers with four or five interns, a licensed veterinary hospital with a veterinarian on staff and a high level of standards and requirements. The staff helps train volunteers and Fitzgerald described the process as a "great learning experience that is very much appreciated by everyone here. We could not do without the volunteers. About 90% are women right now but we are seeing more men come in. I think one of the best things about being a volunteer is that you can see what you accomplish every day. When you're dealing with the rehabilitation of a bird or a turtle you can see the progress and know you are making a difference. That's the satisfaction in being a volunteer."

The Numbers

The hospital serves about 4,000 to 4,500 injured and sick critters a year. A decade ago the mix was 50% birds, 40% mammals and 10% reptiles (mainly box turtles). The past year it was about 65% birds, 30% mammals and 5% reptiles. The process is typical of emergency medical facilities everywhere, beginning with triage then into treatment and ultimately rehabilitation if the bird or animal can be released back into the wild. For those that cannot, Fitzgerald has great sympathy. "If we have to euthanize, it is a more merciful way than leaving the afflicted animal out in the wild. It's never a pleasant choice to have to make but it's better than the alternative."

When Hurricane Ian destroyed Naples Pier the number of hooked and injured birds went down—at least temporarily—but Fitzgerald believes they will come right back up again. What did increase was admissions of gopher tortoises—up a whopping 245% from the prior year.

For the 18 years she has run the facility, she has written a weekly article for the local newspaper. When asked how she managed to keep it interesting for so long she said: "It's just a different story every day. There's a group of people in Naples that love the wildlife and I hear from them all the time about how much they appreciate the stories that I tell. And what am I trying to do? I am trying to educate."

Knowing the Environment

Staff and volunteers at the von Arx Wildlife Hospital also have a unique perspective and understanding of the broader environmental factors reflected in patients that come through the doors. As an example when terns and cormorants are being admitted in greater numbers and the diagnosis is a form of toxicosis it's obvious that red tide is in bloom along the coast. The same applies where staff at the hospital or the veterinarian begins to see clusters caused by bacterial contamination, they know what's going on in the outside world.

Level of Support

As described earlier, the wildlife treatment, rehabilitation and recovery program was on the edge of survival, but when Bill Merrihue began to raise money for the new nature center, he understood how some very well-fixed people felt about it. That level of support continues to this day and Joanna Fitzgerald has a strong opinion. "I think the fact that Sharon and Dolph von Arx's name is on this building says a lot. They are known as among the most general generous philanthropists in southwest Florida. And their support isn't just financial. When Sharon finds an animal or bird in trouble on her property we know about it right away. I remember one case where she had a cormorant in the garage. Now that's a tough bird. It bites. But with her help we captured and brought it in. There's nothing better than the commitment of people like that who put their resources behind their beliefs but aren't afraid to chase a cormorant around the garage."

Future

Despite her jovial and positive nature Fitzgerald is concerned about two things. First is the increase in environmental factors leading to health issues with the wildlife and second is what she calls "geography being stretched." The Conservancy serves an area from Bonita Springs in the north down to Marco Island, but as the eastern part of Collier County grows she's not sure that the Conservancy can meet the needs of receiving and treating injured and impaired wildlife. "It's difficult to deal with some of the gated communities for a couple reasons. First, sometimes we have to get in to pick up wildlife unless it is brought to us and second, we always return rehabilitated birds and animals to the site where we found them. A lot of communities don't want them back again and it's critically important that they be returned to their native habitat in order to forage in familiar territory. The other problem is with all the gates and fences enclosing some of these new subdivisions. The wildlife has no sanctuary; it cannot escape into the wild because there is no wild."

But Fitzgerald has an answer. "We were approached by an individual from Bonita Bay who realized we're pretty far away and suggested we initiate a training program for the staff as to how to handle sick and injured critters. We did that. It has served as a very good model, and now we are introducing the same program at Ave Maria. There we have a committed individual who wanted a similar program in place, and I think that's what it takes. It takes a person with the commitment to see good participation in the training and then to make sure the program is in place and working. And, we have had great success in training community members on Marco Island. I think that will relieve a lot of pressure."

"We are also working proactively on matters like the design of the replacement pier in downtown Naples. Where we can locate emergency equipment to deal with hooked birds is an important matter. Whether or not anyone is paying attention always concerns me, but we did have that one study with the City of Naples on the difference between treble hooks and single hooks. When the city insisted on single hooks we saw a definite decline in injured birds, but we didn't get enough data to draw a definitive conclusion because of storms. That's too bad but is an indication that if we work together we can solve some of the problems."

Contributing to degradation of the natural environment is the increasing number of people and traffic in Lee and Collier counties. Fitzgerald opined on this: "There are so many more people here than when I first came in 1994. There is a noticeable decline in water quality along the coast with red tide and leaking septic tanks. There is a loss of contiguous habitat with the new subdivisions and with the roads and fences and sound barriers that affect the movement of animals and reptiles. The birds are not affected as much because they are able to move freely and adapt, but I do worry about their diet with some of the toxins. Once again it all comes down to education. I feel part of my job is to help people understand how they create problems and how they can contribute, without too much effort, to the solutions. It's all about education and I just hope that some of the people moving here are not just looking for another golf course or another shopping center and learn to appreciate the value of nature in this beautiful part of the world and the creatures that inhabit it." [126]

Education

Along with the Wildlife Hospital, education has been an important and enduring component of the Conservancy's programming package since acquisition of the Big Cypress Nature Center. It has three components: school programs, adult education, and off-site outreach.

School Programs

Many of the school programs are run by Tonya Zadrozny. With a degree in ecological sciences and background of working with eco-tours and the Florida Fish and Wildlife Game Commission, she found that by talking with people about the importance of nature in southwest Florida her career should embrace education, and she joined the Conservancy in 2017 as Student Programs Manager. Many of the activities for which she is responsible are in the classroom from prekindergarten through high school. The Conservancy uses a curriculum that corresponds to the Sunshine State Standards for education, taught by staff, and students' progress is benchmarked as part of the ongoing science curriculum in Collier County schools using the 5-E Learning model, described as: "A formal and informal assessment in which teachers can observe their students and see whether they have a complete grasp of the core concepts. It is also helpful to note whether students approach problems in a different way based on what they learned." [127]

A second iteration is a more intensive after school series, each day with a different theme done on-site or in the field with an emphasis on "hands on" experience, particularly relevant in today's world with the extensive engagement by young people using social media as a proxy for reality.

The Conservancy runs a series of summer programs which tend to be built around a single theme such as invasive species. Again the classes are conducted by staff and interns both on the Conservancy campus and in the field, but were curtailed beginning with the outbreak of COVID in 2018. Programs are planned to start again in 2024 with an optimal size of 16 separated by age categories and once again with a focus on a "hands-on" experience.

Finally, the Conservancy's mobile classroom, known as LAB, allows Conservancy staff to give students the opportunity to participate in research projects taught by both educators and interns.

The curriculum progresses from elementary through middle and high school levels. It begins with an introduction to the species of flora and fauna in southwest Florida and moves on to teach the fundamentals of scientific investigation from population counts and assessments, to the creation of data sets for working hypotheses, leading to eventual correlation and analysis to draw coherent conclusions for further discussion. A lot of the study at the high school level has been centered on subjects of current fascination—like the python and its effect on native ecosystems.

The curriculum, being grade specific, ranges from a 10-minute session in the LAB on pollinators to hour-long programs on environmental issues ranging from harmful algal blooms to invasive species with special emphasis on the python. It is set forth in great detail as to staffing, materials, preparations, content, outlines, and key concepts for each presentation.

One of the more popular offerings is SURVIVORS, in partnership with Rookery Bay, and available for up to 60 students. "The program is designed to engage students in the process of science and incorporates critical thinking, high-level questioning, and scientific techniques. Students will have the opportunity to investigate the impacts of survivorship and have close encounters with estuary residents. The Rookery Bay National Estuarine Research Reserve provides an amazing world for students to discover within its 110,000 acres of pristine mangrove forest, uplands, and protected waters."[128] Access is by the Conservancy's Good Fortune II, allowing students access to the estuary for field work.

Many of the education programs over the last five years have been curtailed due to the outbreak of COVID in 2019. In an interview with Zadrozny and Lori Thorn, Public Programs Manager, the conversation turned to the difficulties of adapting the curriculum and presentation to both the realities and the aftereffects of COVID.

Thorn's degree was as a marine biology major. She began working in a research position in an oncology lab in Miami and became involved in conservation education at the Palm Beach County Nature Center. When her family moved to southwest Florida she ran the Delnor-Wiggins public programs, coming to the Conservancy in 2018. Zadrozny and Thorn work as partners in most of the programs and share similar views, particularly as to the effect of the recent pandemic.

Thorn reflected on the difficulties they both experienced: "When COVID hit we had to move much of our programming to virtual; it became a virtual bandwagon. We had to figure out different ways to do things."[129]

Zadrozny expanded on the point: "We had to make a pivot with the initial shutdown, and now as things reopen we have to make a pivot again but it's not easy. The kids, already tied to their phones, had to place even greater reliance on technology with COVID. What we now have to do is try to provide an immersive experience. There's nothing that replaces that. We are trying to empower kids with the knowledge that gives them the background to make better choices when it comes to how we relate to the natural world. They are going to be our future leaders."

Adult Discovery

The Conservancy runs a number of different programs for adults. There are boat rides down the Gordon River through the mangrove forests with explanatory dialogue by the boat captains as well as kayaks available for people to get out into the river on their own, but the focal point of Conservancy explanatory and visual education is the renovated Dalton Discovery Center.

Upon entering the building the visitor is immediately impressed by a sense of place and the magnitude of the sensory experience. One walks through a series ecosystem ranging from the uplands to the coast and inland to the Everglades, with constructed dioramas and live animal exhibits. Each ecosystem has bright visuals as well as interactive exhibits with explanations available at multiple levels.

Moving through the rooms, a visitor is almost overwhelmed by the presence of lichens and mangroves and cypress trees and water. It is indeed a world apart. An important exhibit demonstrates the functionality of coastal mangroves in buffering against storm surge and how mangrove root systems serve as nature's nurseries from sea grass beds up through the root systems of the walking trees.

Next comes the touch tank—one of the favorites of kids—overseen by staff and interns with a companion exhibit explaining the background and current status of the long-standing sea turtle research project begun by David Addison back in the 1980s.

Walking into the Walter Wing, one is confronted with the many ways invasive species like the python impact native ecosystems by altering the balance of nature in both animals and plants. The python lies coiled and sleeping on a bent palm tree trunk, the exotic cane toad nearly concealed in a grassy plot in front of a shelter and lionfish are swimming slowly around a tank, beautiful but predatory creatures. In that room microscopes are available to help people understand that invasive species are not always large and visible but also at the microscopic level.

Moving through into the next section on climate change is a series of exhibits examining the effect of increasing pH in the water leading to bleaching of the coral reefs, and graphically depicting the increase in salt water intrusion as freshwater aquifers are drawn down. Suspended from the ceiling is an enormous globe illuminated from within, interactive as to the air, water, land and people on the planet. With the press of a button at the control console it comes alive, rotating gradually on the polar axis and displaying any amount of information in dynamic imagery.

The next exhibit goes on to explore the benthic habitat and the creatures living there with a display of trash, plastics and fishing line, and how it affects birds and fish of southwest Florida.

Daily talks are given each day on the outside deck and participants are encouraged to speak their mind. When questioned about how to deal with climate skeptics, Thorn says: "Most of the questions that come are about the validity of research on climate change. Our exhibits don't necessarily deal with the causes as much as the effects, but there is always the question as to why it's happening. There are lot of ingrained opinions but when it comes to adult education, we are always looking forward to that 'aha' moment when we begin to see a change in attitude. It wasn't on climate change but I can recall one instance where we had a group looking at indigenous and exotic snakes. One woman remarked that she had no interest whatsoever in reptiles, but after learning more about their role in southwest Florida's ecosystem, she admitted her attitude had changed. That's the outcome we always hope for."

Both Thorn and Zadrozny are educators who passionately believe that the importance of their work is in creating the wonder of discovery, of giving people the knowledge to enjoy the natural beauty of southwest Florida through a deeper understanding of the importance of preserving native ecosystems, and how to maintain the delicate balance of nature for all the species that call it home, including us.

Education Prevails

The theme of education runs strong in the three women involved in the Conservancy's wildlife hospital, and in the school and adult programs. In every interview the importance of helping people understand how ecosystems function and how people's activities can disrupt them, came into discussion. Fitzgerald spends much of her time thinking about how to prevent injuries to birds and animals through education by means of her weekly column while Thorn and Zadrozny are always trying to find new and better ways to bring people, both young and old, into closer appreciation of nature by being there on the water and in the sand and smelling and listening and touching and carefully studying the living plants and animals so they can develop the fullest sense of appreciation for the larger world about them.

Beyond the Pale

From Highway 941 eastward is a massive area with agricultural activities, pasture and upland forests. It encompasses 232,000 acres of the eastern lands of Collier County. The Conservancy has been deeply involved since 2002 as to how that land is developed, ending up in District Court with a three-year lawsuit settled in July 2023. The eastern lands have two separate but critical water recharge areas one being the Okaloacoochee Slough feeding into populated coastal areas of Collier County.

Moving to the east is the Picayune Strand State Forest. The fourth largest state forest comprises 74,000 acres of wet prairie and cypress swamps, slowly oozing from north to south, cleansing the water and emptying into the 10,000 Islands and Rookery Bay. After being heavily logged in the 1950s, it was purchased, ditched and diked with roads built throughout into a refrigerator tray subdivision. But economics caught up with the Baltimore developers and the area is now being returned to its original state.

Abutting the Picayune is the Fakahatchee Strand with 85,000 acres and the largest concentration of native orchids in North America, including the endangered ghost orchid. It is the largest flow way of water from the Okaloacoochee Slough with multiple species of flora, including a bromeliads, and lakes teeming with wildlife.

The 728,000-acre Big Cypress National Preserve is a gigantic swamp feeding water into part of Everglades National Park. With a flow low gradient, it is home to over a thousand species of vascular flora, dotted with cypress domes. It is a generally unspoiled wilderness with two exceptions: oil wells in the Raccoon Point area and a training airport, once planned to be a major jetport for supersonic passenger planes, but stifled by environmental groups organizing into opposition that even the most hardened politicians had to respect.

These four areas comprise what is essentially the Western Everglades, and today all four are threatened by various means arising from a variety of ideas beginning with a legislative session where local governments were nearly disemboweled, where a simple oversight threatens one of Florida's most precious plants, where the unrelenting press to drill for oil in a national preserve continues, and a serious proposal emerges to build a brand-new airport in a state forest. They display a disheartening reality, threatening a vast watershed. Like a piece of fine tapestry, it depends upon each thread to maintain its identity. These changes are all works in progress. Three have not been fully resolved as of the publication date of this book and the first in the following chapter, a legislative hammer designed to limit the ability of local governments to make and enforce rules germane to their needs, is bound to come back again and again.

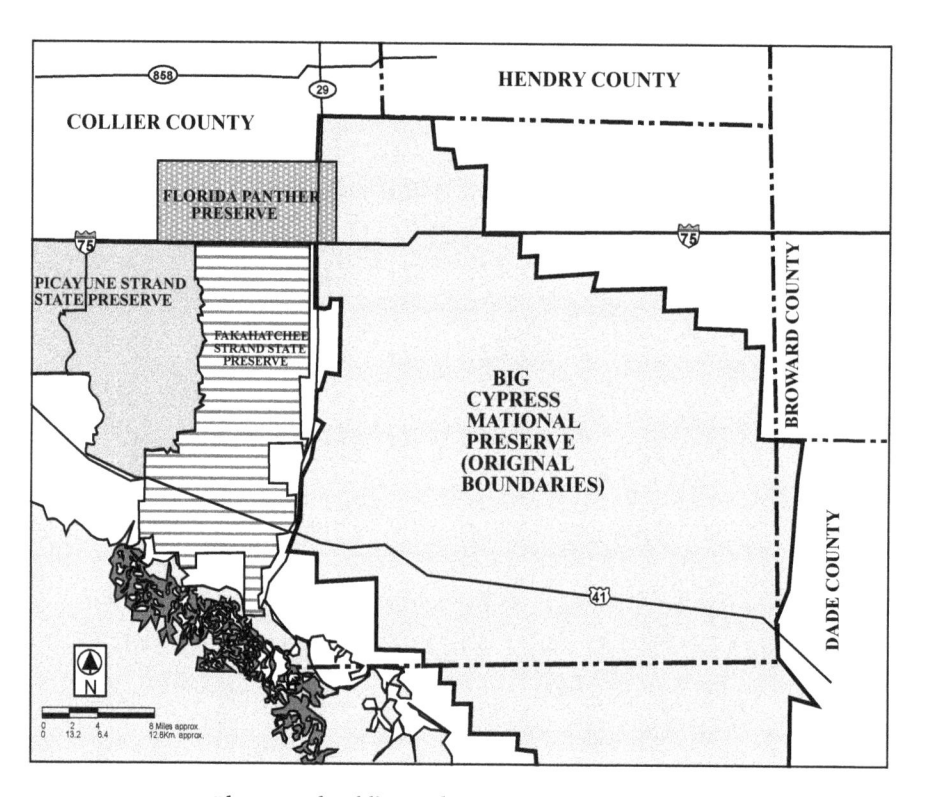

Threatened Public Lands map by: John G. Beriault

Orchids, Oil, and Airports

The 2023 legislative session greased the skids for the development community in the State of Florida. Seven bills were produced, all by members of the party holding a supermajority, with the most notable being HB 1197, known to environmental organizations as the "dirty water bill." More specifically it "prohibits counties and municipalities from adopting laws, regulations, rules, or policies relating to water quality or water quantity, pollution control, discharge prevention or removal, for wetlands and preempts such regulations to the state." The bill also gave the state the ability to withhold funds from any county or city that crosses the line. So much for home rule.

April Olson of the Conservancy noted in a local publication: "If these bills become law, you can expect more harmful algal blooms of blue-green algae and red tide, preserves and wetlands converted to development gridlock, much higher taxes and many of Florida's special places will be gone."[130] The bill died in committee, but the mere fact that it was brought to that level indicated a state of mind of at least one member of the legislature.

In addition there was HB 359 that would permit the prevailing party in a lawsuit to collect all attorneys' fees. With no statewide planning organization place, any challenge that failed in court would end up costing the losing party, preempting almost all citizen challenges. It passed after a few petty amendments and was signed into law by Gov. DeSantis.

The situation in the legislature was simply a reflection of attitudes throughout the state where any cautionary action against the use or abuse of natural resources would be taken from the hands of citizens and shuffled into the maw of the prevailing administration in Tallahassee.

Home of the Ghost

The ghost orchid lives in a very limited range in South Florida including the Big Cypress, Fakahatchee Strand Preserve State Park and Corkscrew Swamp Sanctuary. For years it has been the subject of books, movies, and the target of thieves and poachers who can sell it for extravagant prices. Only 1,500 plants are believed to remain in Florida; less than half of those are old enough to reproduce.

The National Parks Conservation Association, Center for Biological Diversity and the Institute for Regional Conservation petitioned the USFWS reminding the agency that it was legally obligated to perform a review and decide if the species should be listed as either threatened or endangered. The agency was required to make a diligent analysis by January 2023 but missed the deadline and as a result they postponed any further study until the fall of 2026 despite the fact that it was obligated to carry out the review in 2023.

The conservation organizations then filed a lawsuit in September 2023 against the USFWS; the hearing is pending and the outcome uncertain.

Drill Baby Drill in the Big Cypress

Oil exploration in the Big Cypress began in 1939 with a well near Pinecrest on the 40-mile Bend on US 41. Drilling was always preceded by seismic exploration with giant thumper machines running in a straight line across the land and crushing everything along the way.

In quest of a $50,000 prize offered by the governor and cabinet, in 1943 a drilling contractor for Humble Oil Company brought in a producing well in the Big Cypress 12 miles south of Immokalee. It was part of the Sunniland Trend running from Miami northwest and out into the Gulf of Mexico for nearly 200 miles. With the productive zone between 9,000 and 12,000 feet, daily production from Sunniland was a little over 700 barrels a day and additional wells were drilled in the 1970s.

The State of Florida, in 1972, established "Rules and Regulations Governing the Exploration for Hydrocarbons in the Big Cypress Area" requiring permits and monitoring of exploration activities and drilling in the region. The regulations were in response to concerns expressed by the public, mainly hunters, and led to formation of the Big

Cypress Advisory Committee (BCSAC) formed by Gov. Reubin Askew. The committee had direct access to the governor and cabinet without having to work through the bureaucracy of other agencies and because of that it was highly effective.

That same year, Humble Oil discovered additional reserves at Bear Island, just southeast of Sunniland.

The Big Cypress was created as a National Preserve two years later and in 1976 the Collier family conveyed almost 77,000 acres to the National Park Service. As part of the transaction and transfer of property, a number of hunting and grazing rights were grandfathered recognizing the historic relationship of the Seminole and Miccosukee people but mineral rights remained in the hands of the Collier family.

In 1976 a road was permitted and constructed to run from US 41 north to an exploratory area at Raccoon Point. The trend was producing 14,000 barrels per day at the time and a year later a Humble wildcat hit oil and began producing. To get the oil to a refinery, it was pumped by a 4,000-foot pipeline to the Miccosukee Reservation north of I-75. From there it's loaded onto trucks and then transported to Port Everglades and eventually barged to refineries along the Gulf Coast. The Sunniland crude from Raccoon Point and other wells has high sulfur content and only a few refineries are able to crack it.

Six years later the National Park Service decided to remove the existing road and build one to replace it, running south from SR 84 (now I-75) down to the well field. It would've been 16 miles long, 11 miles in the Big Cypress but the BCSAC, studying the matter, recommended denial of the permit and the road was never built. In a letter to Gov. Bob Graham, the executive director of the Florida Game and Fresh Water Fish Commission made a strong case that the road would have a dramatic impact on the Florida panther. But buried in the letter, and more to the point: "There is no comprehensive plan for long-range development of access associated with mineral production in the area; therefore, roads and field development plans are considered on a piecemeal basis."[131] As true today as it was 40 years ago.

In 1990 the Collier family agreed to sell an additional 83,000 acres to the National Park Service for the Addition Lands expansion of the Big Cypress, but as in all transactions reserved the right to explore and extract minerals.[132]

Exploratory activities since 1992 have been conducted using 3-D seismic surveys. They employ vibroseis vehicles that pound the surface as they move to give subsurface readings that geologists then use to identify and calculate reserves. Traveling through wetlands they leave ruts up to two feet deep and damage wildlife habitat and natural vegetation in their travel lanes.[133]

Subject to almost constant criticism, in 2002 the Collier families agreed to sell mineral rights to the government for $120 million, but the deal was scotched after a careful look at how the price was arrived at with little or no attention to federal experts.

Drilling was always a matter of price, and the cost of building infrastructure in a swamp and getting equipment and crude in and out was always a consideration. The price of oil was gyrating; in 2008 with the global financial collapse it reached $125 a barrel but the following year dropped dramatically to less than $50, but by 2012 with prices rising again toward $100 the Hughes Oil Company reached an agreement with Collier Resources Company (CRC) to begin drilling.

Then, disaster struck. In early 2014 Hughes was fined $25,000 by the Florida Department of Environmental Protection (FDEP) "for injecting unapproved acid into Florida's vulnerable underground limestone formations in the middle of Audubon Society's Corkscrew Swamp Sanctuary, a major nesting site for wood storks." The company had a permit to use acid stimulation but decided to go one step beyond the permit and "injected a proprietary, high-pressure mix of sand and chemical gel, called a 'proppant,' to keep the fractured limestone open to help ease the flow of oil." [134]

The Hughes Company had enough and shut the project down, but continued pumping with another well called the Collier-Hogan 20-3H, important because it generated a good data set from which FDEP, in 2015, issued a finding that regulated hydraulic fracturing fluids, released at the depth of the well (14,365 feet), could not have risen to the level of the shallow freshwater aquifers, concluding that acid stimulation into the highly porous limestone karst substrata of Florida would not cause adverse impact on the higher-level aquifers.

But the damage was done with the situation at Corkscrew. Environmental organizations—notably the Conservancy—cast a wary eye on further exploration. And that was about to take place with the Burnett Oil Company contracting with CRC to do seismic testing in the Big Cypress.

In 2017 and 2018 the Texas-based company, using 33-ton vibroseis vehicles thumping through over 100 miles of upland and wetlands, left huge ruts and over 500 Cypress trees either run over or cut down. The Conservancy had been resisting further exploration in the federal courts since 2016, and had been in constant contact with FDEP every year, requesting that it review the 2016 permit issued to Burnett with regard to its mitigation plan to revegetate impacted areas and fully restore the ruts to pre-survey condition.

For future seismic surveys, the Conservancy "participated in settlement negotiations with FDEP in 2017-2018 and as a result there were some more detailed and thoughtful permit conditions in the FDEP's oil and gas permit for Burnett's continued seismic survey, including how the damage would be reclaimed, restored, and mitigated."[135]

Collier Resources, jointly owned by the two branches of the family, maintains that best management practices are in place and are effectively enforced with its contractors. The company attempts to limit the size of well pads, and pledges to use existing roads and trails for construction and access, and to "restore impacted areas back to their native condition."[136]

Despite those assurances, still on the CRC website, the damage done by the Burnett Company was not fully repaired and the Conservancy with its partners, found itself once again pleading for a tougher and enforced restoration plan, this time addressing a letter to the National Park Service (NPS) superintendent, Tom Forsyth. "What we are engaging in now is a NEPA review associated with the new drilling proposals. Burnett has two sites within Big Cypress that would require new oil pads and new roads that they have submitted to NPS for consideration. We have been told that NPS intends to do a NEPA EIS for these proposals. Of course we have been pointing out the bad history of Burnett's lingering damage with the seismic survey, and continued gaps in meeting their permitting requirements, as cause for denying their oil drilling proposals. We haven't heard anything recently about when NPS will take official comments on the EIS; we submitted our comments in February 2022 proactively."[137]

The end game for environmental groups is a buyout of the mineral rights in the Big Cypress. After falling apart in 2002 over the issue of valuation, it came up again 20 years later when Wildlandscapes International negotiated a tentative agreement with Collier Resources to purchase the rights to almost 320,000 acres in the Preserve and the Florida Panther National Wildlife Refuge. Money would come from the federal Land and Water Conservation Fund with Wildlandscapes working an intermediary between the company and the government. The Miccosukee Tribe is also involved in attempting to preserve their native land, and there appears to be bipartisan support in the Congress. [138]

With the Hamas invasion of Israel, the price artificially low during the global pandemic, is rising once again to over $80 a barrel. Valuation of the mineral rights depends upon an accurate estimate of the acreage containing available reserves as well as an estimate of the price of crude over time. Collier Resources is run by people who make decisions based on business principles, so if a fair offer is made it will likely be accepted.

Naples Airport in the Picayune Strand

Among the panoply of bad ideas to recently emerge, this one simply defies the imagination. The idea began in June 2023 when Environmental Science Associates (ESA) was selected to do an initial presentation, in terms of scope and fee, for an exploratory study to relocate the Naples Airport.

In September 2023, Robert Burns, a retired architect and urban planner and recently appointed Commissioner of the Naples Airport Authority, asked its director, Chris Rozansky, to distribute a series of three aerial maps showing how the airport could be relocated to the Picayune Strand, once Southern Golden Gate Estates, and now in the final steps of full restoration to its natural condition as part of the Comprehensive Everglades Restoration Program (CERP).

Burns got his idea after "a conversation with a Naples resident who has firsthand knowledge of the approval of construction of Hamilton Harbor by the Florida Department of Environmental Protection, after it was initially rejected."[139] That was followed in a memo on Authority stationery by a remarkable sentence. "Both believe a similar justification would lead to approval of a new airport in a state forest."[140] An obvious conclusion would be that both the "Naples resident," and more importantly FDEP, believed this to be a realistic alternative.

At its October meeting, a $438,000 contract with ESA was approved with a general scope of work for the first phase including aviation needs, facility requirements, high level cost estimates, and identification of potential new airport sites.

At the meeting Michelle Arquette-Palermo restated the Conservancy's position. "At last month's meeting our policy director, Nicole Johnson, requested that Picayune Strand be removed from any further consideration as a potential location. I would like to reiterate that point by updating you on the status of the Picayune restoration project. Last week the removal of 285 miles of road and pavement was completed. Final canal filling will begin in January. Native plants and animals are returning to the area, including the wood stork and the endangered Florida Panther. As previously stated, you would be hard-pressed to find a less appropriate location to consider for an airport."[141]

Once the Picayune Strand was identified, Rozansky walked it back as fast as he could. Quoted in the *Naples Daily News*, he referred back to a 1990s study remarking that it never got to the "site identification stage." He then referred to another study completed in June 2019 at a cost of $2 million having to do with noise abatement, then concluded by commenting that he thought it was "healthy for a growing county to look at its long-term preservation plan."[142]

Burns idea may have originated with a former employee of Wilson Miller (now Stantec), the company involved in representing Collier Enterprises in the battle over Sabal Bay and Hamilton Harbor that ended up in court for almost 13 years. Supporting this was an addendum on the back of the Rozansky memo that sets out in great detail the work of Wilson Miller and contains the following notes. "How does it help us with the relocation of the existing Naples airport? Picayune Strand State Forest—A New Site for Naples Airport; duplicate identical rationale used at Hamilton Harbor."[143]

But to equate it with a new airport was a vacuous argument. Hamilton Harbor was originally tied in to a 2,400-acre development called Sabal Bay. It ended up being a coastal marina with a powerboat fueling station and storage for smaller boats to take pressure off north Naples Bay. It was a little over 100 acres in its final incarnation, part of it remaining as mangrove fringe forests and conservation land. It was a result of a negotiated settlement agreeable to all parties—something that would never happen when trying to build an airport in a state forest and in the first fully completed CERP project.

Midnight Raid on Conservation Collier

The last case is a done deal (maybe).

In three separate ballots beginning in 2002, voters approved an ad valorem tax to fund Conservation Collier, a program administered by an independent board to acquire and maintain land with desirable natural resources. The most recent vote in November 2020 garnered 151,000 votes for a 77% approval rate despite the Republican County Committee opposing the measure.

But Collier County Commission chairman Rick LoCastro was having none of it. "I was surprised with the large percentage of which it passed. A lot of times, that percentage is used as evidence that citizens love the project. But if this room was full of people that passed it, I'll just throw it out there, I think sometimes when you read one or two lines on a ballot. When you sit down and do the math, I think there's a percentage of people who might go, oh, I didn't realize that." [144]

He, and three others, ended up voting early in the morning of October 10, 2023, to take approximately $60 million from the maintenance fund to balance the budget and to use for their own purposes. Anticipated tax receipts would have risen by $62 million with the increase in property values throughout the county, but the commission decided that would amount to a "tax increase" and decided instead to raid the maintenance fund.

They had the support of the county attorney, Jeff Klatzow. Once again, according to the commission chair: "We have a county attorney that keeps us legal, moral and ethical. And we look to his judgment and guidance. And so I think he has been very clear. And what we are allowed to do could be unique, could be something that was unexpected, but it's not illegal, immoral or unethical." [145] The public trust was never mentioned and while there was some idle chatter about replenishing the maintenance fund there was no action taken to do so.

Funds taken were in a trust established for maintenance of acquired lands, so there were raised eyebrows when the county attorney gave the raid a green light, and the issue still percolated after the 4-1 vote. But Klatzow had an answer. Amend the ordinance that created Conservation Collier retroactively to allow the County Commission to appropriate funds as it pleased. Once again, the public trust was never mentioned and both the county attorney and commissioners have refused to comment further as of the publication date of this book.

Redux

The five cases cited above represent aspects too common in today's world. Overriding local authority and practices, a simple act of negligence, and two proposals to forever alter the balance of nature in public lands. They speak to an onset of authoritarianism where money and power dominate, and where the will of the people is blithely ignored.

Final Thoughts at 60

What follows is taken from a series of conversations with Rob Moher, chief executive officer of the Conservancy during the past decade. The text had been reviewed by him but any modifications he suggested were carefully reviewed and remain the work of the author.

Rob Moher began his career in Canada. He worked in policy for the International Development Research Center with a focus on global conservation. With a master's degree in international environmental issues, he moved from there with his family to a broader job with the Bahamas National Trust, where he developed his skills in fundraising and advocacy.

He admitted that coming to the Conservancy temporarily narrowed his career path. "The Conservancy offered me an opportunity to join a multifaceted organization. I was initially involved in fundraising, because I understood that all not-for-profits needed to be nourished regularly to be sustainable, so was happy to lend my skills to that aspect of the organization." Then a vice president position opened up, allowing him to expand his role into marketing while continuing with development, leading to a feasibility study for the $38 million capital campaign in 2009–2011. "Kathy Prosser leaned on me a lot. We talked about strategy, board management, governance, and a number of other things. She gave me the opportunity to further broaden my role within the organization."

When Andrew McElwaine came to the Conservancy, Moher continued to function in much the same role. "Andrew was all about policy and left to me the marketing and messaging and governance and development. Then, when he left to go to the American Farmland Trust the job of president and CEO opened up, and frankly as I looked at the hours involved I thought it was almost too much. But I think it was Dave Schindle who really convinced me to apply for the job. He said 'Rob, you need to do this. The science team is behind you and we really hope you will step up and apply for this position.' In the interview process with the search committee Phil Gresh, the chair, leaned across the table and looked me in the eye and said 'we are concerned about your ability to carry the message on policy.' I responded that my background in the earlier years of my career was all about policy so I was entirely comfortable with that aspect of the job."

That same day, the search committee offered Moher the position of president & CEO. From his first day on the job, he understood that building trust was the best way to establish an effective and collaborative culture, paramount to his ability to grow the organization to the next level of success.

With the assistance of former board chair Bob Heidrick's widow Raynelle, he connected with Dave Fleming, a mentor who believed that "culture eats strategy for breakfast" as author Peter Drucker once said. Fleming became an indispensable ally in the work of shaping the values of the organization that Moher was forging.

Moher's philosophy is straightforward. "It begins with family. I always put family first and told that to the search committee. The board knows this too and has always had my back. I feel my job is to empower staff. I am basically the chief obstacle remover. I have a great staff and can easily turn things over to them at any time and know that they will manage it quickly and effectively, so I don't have to micromanage the organization. They all know what to do and how to do it, so I trust them implicitly." [146]

When talking about the future, he is very specific. "One of the big problems we face is land valuation. The cost of an acre of land anywhere in Collier and Lee County has skyrocketed. Workforce housing is sorely lacking and the question is how can developers buy the land at current prices, build good homes and apartments, and make enough money. They simply are not willing to do so. And it's because they make a lot more money by building in the higher end of the market. Then look at what the County Commission just did to Conservation Collier by grabbing the maintenance fund for their own uses. They defied the will of people who voted 77% in the last reauthorization round to tax themselves for the purpose of buying land for conservation, but the commissioners decided they knew better how to spend the money. It's all related. Southwest Florida is growing and pressures are increasing on public infrastructure. If we hope to maintain our quality of life in some way, local government and elected officials should be focused on slowing and shaping growth in a more sustainable manner, as opposed to fast-tracking it without proper planning. The temptation to use preserved lands for non-conservation purposes is growing and this will continue to be an area where we can't let our guard down."

Moher continued. "We do a lot of work on the effects of climate change on our coast and communities. Look at temperatures in the Gulf of Mexico this year. They were extraordinarily high. Climate change is going to impact a lot of people who live and work here. It's not going to affect the mostly affluent, they come here eager to play golf for a few weeks and then leave. This isn't where they live; it's where they visit. That's not true of everyone, like the founders of the Conservancy who 60 years ago were concerned and engaged like our members and directors are today, but there are some people who simply don't care about the long-term wellbeing of our community as much. We work hard to change that attitude by creating an appreciation of the natural world and our relationship to it. That's not always easy but it's what we do. We seek to provide solutions, not just opposition to the challenging issues. We work on nature-based solutions from a series of very good data sets. We know a lot about things like wetlands and pythons, but the most important thing we have is our independence. We are not influenced by anything other than our mission and we remain completely apolitical in the sense of parties and candidates. And I have a great staff and a great board and a great family. What more can you want?" [147]

ENDNOTES

[1] Merged into the Department of Natural Resources in 1969.

[2] *Naples Daily News*, April 27, 1967.

[3] There are four of the twelve snook varieties found off the coast of Florida. The largest, most populous and best studied is the common snook.

[4] Fry are juvenile fish of any species; the word fry is not scientifically explicit.

[5] Harmon Shields, (executive director, Florida Department of Natural Resources) to Breaux Ballard (Chairman, Conservancy Fishing Committee), May 27, 1975.

[6] Dale Beaumarriage (Chief, Bureau of Marine Science and Technology, Department of Natural Resources) to Willard Merrihue, June 14, 1976.

[7] Memo "Summary of First 1986 Snook Capture Effort," Ed Johanson, June 11, 1986.

[8] Ed Johanson (Special Projects Director, The Conservancy) to Jerry Bruger (Florida Department of Natural Resources), July 7, 1987.

[9] Optimal foraging theory holds that birds, fish and mammals will naturally seek out the greatest caloric intake with the lowest caloric expenditure of effort to capture prey.

[10] Collier County Mosquito Control District History, March 7, 2007.

[11] *Florida Sportsman*, January 1985.

[12] *Ibid.*

[13] *Florida Sportsman*, id.

[14] *Naples Daily News*, June 6, 1985.

[15] One study cited by the American Bird Conservancy showed that starlings died within five seconds of sitting on a Rid-a-Bird perch with fenthion pasted on it. The mortality rate was in the 70% range.

[16] Under increasing pressure from conservationists, in March 2003, the manufacturer agreed to pull the chemical from the market and the U.S. Environmental Protection Agency ruled that all sales and applications of Baytex must cease by November 30, 2004.

[17] David Addison, interview with the author, January 24, 2014.

[18] Widmer, Randolph: The Evolution of the Calusa. Tuscaloosa: University of Alabama Press, 1988. p.7.

[19] MacMahon and Marquardt, p.44.

[20] Murphy, J.M.: Turtling in Florida, Harper's Weekly 1890.

[21] Hendriksen, John R. The Ecological Strategies of Sea Turtles. American Zoology 20: pp. 597-607.

[22] *Ibid.*

[23] *Ibid.*

[24] Garman, Samuel. On A Certain Species of Chelonioida. Bulletin undated.

[25] David Addison, interview with the author, January 6, 2012.

[26] Ross Obley worked with Bill Merrihue to build the large Pelican Bay development to high environmental standards.

[27] The "Headstart" experiment was attempted by a small number of organizations worldwide, but abandoned when researchers found that released animals were not behaving as normally as those allowed to grow in the wild.

[28] Most southwest Florida municipalities have passed statutes limiting coastal lighting during turtle nesting season—generally from May to November.

[29] David Addison, interview with the author, January 6, 2012.

[30] Rudloe, p. 81.

[31] Gore, Robert H.: The Gulf of Mexico. Sarasota: Pineapple Press, 1997. p.172.

[32] David Addison, *Ibid.*

[33] Steve Bortone, "State of the Environmental Science Division—Report to Conservancy Board of Directors," February 2, 2000.

[34] See Kathy Worley, Mangroves and an Indicator of Estuarine Conditions in Restoration Areas in Bortone, ed.

[35] Kathy Worley and Vanessa Booher: Clam Bay Mangrove Assessment Project 1999–2022. Conservancy of Southwest Florida: January, 2023.

[36] Interview with Kathy Worley, April 11 2023.

[37] Kathy Worley interview with the author April 11, 2023.

[38] Ronald L. Myers and John J. Ewel: Ecosystems of Florida. University of Central Florida Press, Orlando, 1990: p. 546.

[39] Armentano, T. V., R. A. Park, and C. L. Cloonan. The effect of future sea level rise on U.S. Coastal Wetland Areas. Final report to U.S. Environmental Protection Agency, Butler University, Indianapolis: 1986

[40] Kathy Worley interview with the author April 11, 2023.

[41] Reed, R.N., and Rodda, G.H., 2009, Giant constrictors: Biological and management profiles and an establishment risk assessment for nine large species of pythons, anacondas, and the boa constrictor: U.S. Geological Survey, Open-File Report 2009.

[42] Guzy, Jacquelyn et al. Burmese pythons in Florida: A Synthesis of Biology, Impacts, and Management Tools: NeoBiota. 80.

[43] A morph is a particular pattern or color trait that shows itself in a snake. Once breeders have identified certain genetic lines that carry these they can carefully select for them. Certain morphs can be reliably bred and sold to consumers a few generations later.

[44] John D. Willson: Indirect effects of invasive Burmese pythons on Ecosystems in southern Florida, Journal of Applied Ecology, August 2017.

[45] Spencer Dudley, PhD et al.: 2022 – 2023 Collier County Community Assessment. QQ Research Consultants, Miami Florida.

[46] Florida Population 1900-2022, *Macro Trends*.

[47] Taken directly from Florida Department of Community Affairs Company Profile, Tallahassee, FL, *Competitors, Financials & Contacts from Dun & Bradstreet* (www.dnb.com)

[48] According to www.mitigationbankinginc.com,"FLUCCS codes are a system of land use and cover classification used widely in Florida. They are used by environmental managers and regulatory agencies to identify and describe the current and proposed land use and cover of an area."

[49] The base value to qualify would be 1.2.

[50] The value under the index system would be 1.5.

[51] Rev. F.S. 163. 3177 (11) (d).

[52] Formed under the Florida Special Purpose Local Government Act, the district would be run by a five-person Board of Supervisors initially nominated and elected by the landowners. They were empowered to provide for utilities construct roads bridges maintain wildlife habitat areas build out recreational health and public safety facilities, to operate public transportation, pest control, and to build schools all financed by bonds funded through truces, special assessments, and user fees. The expectation was that the supervisory board would transition to local residents over time.

[53] According to one report, in July 2023 the median listing price in Naples was $847,500 and in Miami $6651000. *Naples Daily News:* July 71 2023.

[54] https://www.newsweek.com/February 6, 2023

[55] https://rollcall.com/December 10, 2018

56 The RFMUD is about 77,000 acres east of Collier Boulevard.

57 In the interest of full disclosure the author was an at-large member of the committee during its entire term and chair during the last two years.

58 Notes from: Meeting Summary for RLSA Restudy Group 3 Policies Meeting—Protecting Natural Resources April 26, 2018C p. 10.

59 Minutes of review/input: Group 1 and other policies RLSA restudy meeting, January 31, 2019, p. 6.

60 *Naples Daily News*, July 4, 2017.

61 Minutes, Board of County Commissioners meeting October 22, 2019, p.168.

62 *Ibid.*, p. 213

63 *Ibid.*, p. 214

64 *Ibid.*, p. 212

65 Collier County Rural Lands Stewardship Area Overlay Restudy White Paper, May 2019, p. 68.

66 Collier County Rural Lands Stewardship Area Overlay Restudy White Paper, May 2019, p. 68.

67 Collier Enterprises website: *Rivergrass*.

68 *Gulf Shore Business*, July 30, 2023.

69 www.https://colliernesa.com/faqs.

70 Judith M. Hushon and Lynn S. Martin, *Naples Daily News*, October 29, 2020.

71 Dover, Kohl and Partners for Collier County: "Toward Better Places, the Community Character Plan for Collier County, Florida." April 2001.

72 Collier Development was another subsidiary of Collier Enterprises.

73 Florida Rev. Statutes 2022: Title XI, Sec. 163.3248.

74 https://www.naplesnews.com/story/news/environment/2020/04/07/rivergrass-village-lawsuit-collier-enterprises-joins-countys-side-lawsuit/2960109001/

75 https://www.naplesnews.com/story/news/environment/2020/04/07/rivergrass-village-lawsuit-collier-enterprises-joins-countys-side-lawsuit/2960109001/

76 Circuit Court 20th Judicial Circuit In and For Collier County. Conservancy of Southwest Florida Inc. vs. Collier County Florida and Collier Enterprises Management Inc. Case number: 11-20-CA-000780-0001.

77 *Ibid.*

78 *Ibid.*

79 *Ibid.*

80 *Ibid.*

81 District Court of Appeal Second District of Florida, Conservancy of Southwest Florida vs. Collier County, Florida and Collier Enterprises Management Inc. Case N2D21-2094. December 2, 2022.

82 *Ibid.*

83 *Naples Daily News,* December 2, 2022

84 https://conservancy.org/settlement-reached-on-rivergrass-village/

85 *Naples Daily News,* June 10, 2020

86 www.https://skysailflorida.com. More recently the development's website states that prices will start in the "low $500s."

87 This story was covered extensively in an article in *Gulf Shore Business* in partnership with the Florida Center for Government Accountability. April 20, 2021.

88 Letter to Megan Mills, Florida Department of Environmental Protection, Robert Kerry, division lead for environmental review. U.S. Fish and Wildlife Service, Jason Height, director, Office of Conservation Planning Services, Florida Fish and Wildlife Conservation Commission, February 17, 2022.

89 *Ibid.*

90 www. wildbluefl.com

91 www.conservancy.org.

92 Clem, Shawn and Michael Duever: Hydrologic Changes over 60 years (1959-2019) in an Old Growth Bald Cypress Swamp on a Rapidly Developing Landscape. *Wetland Science and Practice,* October 2019.

93 https://news.bloomberglaw.com/environment. Bobby Magill: DeSantis' Big Bet on Florida's EPA Takeover Isn't Paying Off. *Environment & Energy,* April 18, 2023.

94 Frakes et al., 2015. Landscape Analysis of Adult Florida Panther Habitat. PLoS ONE 10(7): e0133044. doi:10.1371/journal.pone.0133044.

95 The author, having observed Crested Caracara nesting activity in Collier County, can attest to the birds' high level of sensitivity to movement within the forest and for the need to be quiet near the nest.

[96] Letter from Julianne Thomas to Jennifer Carpenter, Director of District Management Florida Department of Environmental Protection, dated June 21, 2023.

[97] *Ibid.*

[98] https://bloomberglaw.com. *Ibid.*

[99] https://floridadep.gov/water/submerged-lands-environmental resources-coordination/content/state-404-program#.

[100] Chapter 62-331, Florida Administrative Code (F.A.C.)

[101] Chapter 62-330, (F.A.C.).

[102] Letter from Karimah Schoenhut, Staff Attorney Sierra Club, to Roxana Hinzman, Field Supervisor U.S. Fish and Wildlife Service, September 9, 2020.

[103] *Ibid.*

[104] ECPO was an organization formed by Barron Collier Companies and Collier Enterprises that included Alico Land Development, Gargiulo, Consolidated Citrus Limited Partnership, Half Circle L Ranch LLP, Heller Brothers Packing Corp., Sunniland Family Limited Partnership, Owl Hammock Immokalee LLC and Pacific Land LTD.

[105] Amber Crooks note to author, October 26, 2023.

[106] Letter from Bonnie Malloy, Earthjustice to Kelly Laycock, Oceans, Wetlands and Streams Protection Branch EPA Region Four dated October 23, 2020

[107] https://floridadep.gov/water/submerged-lands-environmental resources-coordination/content/state-404-program#.

[108] https://conservancy.org/wp-content/uploads/2021/12/CSWFL-39451- Flyer-03-404-Program.

[109] Amber Crooks note to author October 26, 2023.

[110] State 404 Program Annual Report July 1, 2021 – June 30, 2022. Division of Water Resource Management, Florida Department of Environmental Protection, pp 8 – 9.

[111] This topic is covered extensively in *Nature's Steward: A History of the Conservancy of Southwest Florida* published by Pineapple Press, 2014.

[112] The Pacific Legal Foundation, based in Sacramento California, carefully disguises most of its funding. However, according to various sources, among supporters are the Koch brothers Exxon Mobil Corporation and the conservative Scaife family of Pittsburgh.

[113] https://www.miami.gov/My-Government/ClimateChange/King-Tides.

[114] *Smithsonian*, November-December, 2022, p. 101

[115] The berm is seaward and protects the dunes to mitigate the effects of wind and surge.

[116] https://usace.contentdm.oclc.org/utils/getfile/collection/p16021coll7/id/14939, p. ii.

[117] https://conservancy.org/wp-content/uploads/2023/06/6-7-23-Conservancy-Collier-CSRM-Comment-Letter.

[118] https://conservancy.org/the-army-corps-coastal-storm-risk-management-csrm-study-is-off-to-a-great-start/.

[119] https://www.nature.org/content/dam/tnc/nature/en/documents/Mangrove_Report_digital_FINAL. p. 5.

[120] *Ibid.*, p. 12

[121] U.S. Army Corps of Engineers, Norfolk District. *Draft Integrated Feasibility Study and Environmental Impact Statement.* Collier County, Florida Coastal Storm Risk Management. July 2020.

[122] https://floridastateparksfoundation.org/wp-content/uploads/2022/05/Delnor-Wiggins-Pass-State-Park.

[123] https://ewn.erdc.dren.mil/nbs-guidance/

[124] Rob Moher, November 7, 2023

[125] Kathy Worley, November 7, 2023

[126] The author feels there is no need for endnotes in this chapter since all quotes were taken directly from conversations with Joanna Fitzgerald.

[127] https://lesley.edu/article/empowering-students-the-5e-model-explained

[128] Tonya Zadrozny, email to the author, October 31, 2023.

[129] Author's interview with Thorn and Zadrozny, October 26, 2023. Here again, the author has not inserted endnotes into many of the quotes since the source is identified in the text.

[130] *Florida Weekly*, March 16, 2023.

[131] Robert M. Brantly to the Hon. Bob Graham, October 21, 1982.

[132] The deal actually included 108,000 acres; about 25,000 acres would become the Florida Panther National Wildlife Refuge.

[133] www.earthisland.org/journal/index.php/articles/entry/wildcat-wells-in-florida-big-cypress-preserve.

[134] https://oilprice.com/energy/energy/General/oil-company-ordered-to-halt-illegal-operation-near-florida-panther-preserve.

[135] Amber Crooks, email to the author, October 31, 2023.

[136] www.collierresources.com/operating-standards-management-practices

[137] Amber Crooks, email to the author, October 31, 2023.

[138] For an interesting perspective on this please see Kristine Gill, "Conservation Groups Seeking to End Decades of Drilling in Big Cypress," *Gulf Shore Business*, September 1, 2023

[139] Christopher A. Rozansky, Executive Director, in a memo to Hon. Chair and Commissioners, September 21, 2023.

[140] *Ibid.*

[141] Notes by Michele Arquette-Palermo, Water Policy Manager Conservancy of Southwest Florida, October 19, 2023.

[142] Kyle Foster, "Naples Airport Authority to study move to east Collier County," *Naples Daily News*, October 24, 2023.

[143] Rozansky, *Ibid.*

[144] Minutes from Collier County Board of Commissioners meeting, September 21, 2023.

[145] *Ibid.*

[146] Rob Moher interview with author February 23, 2023.

[147] *Ibid.*, October 26, 2023.

INDEX

A

Addison, Dave 20-22, 24, 30, 36, 40, 46, 176
APA (Administrative Procedures Act)............................. 141
Ave Maria... 70-72, 85, 90, 170

B

Barron Collier Companies 67, 70
Bartozek, Ian 47-53, 55-57
Bellmar...74, 83, 86-87, 89, 93
Benedict, Mark 20-21, 38, 46
Bert Harris claim 125
Big Cypress National Preserve 50, 93, 181

C

Calusa 23, 104
Camp Keais Strand 75, 87, 110, 112, 115
Clam Bay 39-40, 42-44, 92
Collier Enterprises... 67, 72-73, 83, 85-90, 92-93, 95, 97-98, 102-103, 193
Conservation Collier................................ 78, 110, 194-195
Corps (U.S. Army Corps of Engineers).......................10, 33, 45, 58, 60, 120-121, 124, 131-133, 139-141, 143, 146, 148-151, 154, 156, 157-158, 161-162
CREW (Corkscrew Regional Ecosystem Watershed) . 87, 106, 108-112, 115, 119, 129
Crooks, Amber..108, 136, 138, 142
CSRM (Coastal Storm Risk Management)........... 150-151, 156, 161
CWA (Clean Water Act)............................132, 135, 144, 146

210

D

DCA (Department of Community Affairs) 63-64, 69, 75, 80, 158
DeSantis, Gov. Ron. 135, 139, 184
DNR (Department of Natural Resources) 7, 16-17
DR/GR (Density Reduction/Groundwater Recharge) 109, 112-119, 121, 130

E

Earthjustice 134, 137, 138, 139
ECPO (Eastern Collier Property Owners). 108, 136, 141-142
EEPCO (Environmental Enhancement and Preservation Communities Overlay) 127-128
EIS (Environmental Impact Statement) 136, 190
Environmental Impact Statement 136
EPA (Environmental Protection Agency) . 124-125, 131-133, 135-136, 140, 145-146
ERP (Environmental Resource Permit) 133-134, 143
ESA 141

F

Fakahatchee Strand 115, 181, 184
FDEP (Florida Department of Environmental Protection) 109, 124, 129, 131-134, 135, 136, 139-140, 142, 144, 188-189, 192
FFD (Florida Farms Development). 114, 119, 125-126, 128
Fitzgerald, Joanna 165-170, 178
FRC (Five-year Review Committee) ...69-70, 75, 77, 80-81, 84-85, 104

G

GMP (Growth Management Plan). 64, 67, 69-70, 77, 80, 82, 92, 95, 98, 100-102, 106, 108
Graham, Gov. Bob 19, 62-63, 70, 99, 187
Green Sea Turtle. 25, 32

211

H

Hawksbill 26
HCP (Habitat Conservation Plan) 74, 86, 135-136, 141-142
Hyde Park Village 89, 105

I

Immokalee 75-77, 81, 107, 112, 185
Immokalee Road Rural Village 106

J

Johnson, Nicole 78, 91, 95, 102, 141, 153, 192

K

Kemp's ridley 26, 30-32, 35
Key Island 25, 27-29, 35-36
Kingston 114, 119, 126-128, 130-131

L

LAAC (Land Acquisition Advisory Council) 110
LDC (Land Development Code) 67, 82, 92, 106
Leatherback 25-26, 157
Loggerhead 24-27, 32-34, 157
Longwater 83, 86-87, 89-90, 93

M

Merrihue, Bill 163-165, 168
Moher, Rob 57, 59, 92, 95, 161, 197-200
MPO (Metropolitan Planning Organization) 65, 89, 91, 123, 128

N

National Panther Wildlife Refuge 87

212

NEPA (National Environmental Policy Act).... 120-121, 136, 141, 190
NRI (Natural Resource Index) 65, 79

O

Okaloacoochee Slough................................ 75, 93, 180-181
Olson, April 79, 91, 95, 105, 152-153, 153, 156, 183

P

Picayune Strand 48, 180, 191-193

R

RFMUD (Rural Fringe Mixed Use District)........................ 76-77
Rivergrass 83, 86-87, 89, 91, 93, 95-99, 102-104
RLSA (Rural Lands Stewardship Area)........ 64, 66, 75-76, 79-80, 96, 103-104
Rob   197
RPC (Regional Planning Council) 73

S

Sabal Bay 17, 94, 193
Sakata Farms 122
Schmelz, Gary 28, 29, 163-164
Schmid, Jeff 31, 34-37
Scott, Gov. Rick 75, 80, 131-132, 139, 158
SFWMD (South Florida Water Management District)..... 33, 110, 124
Sierra Club.. 104, 135, 137
SRA (Stewardship Receiving Area)................ 67, 71, 77, 89-90, 96
SSA (Stewardship Sending Area).......................... 65, 67-68, 71
Stewardship Receiving Area 67

213

T

Thorn, Lori 175, 177-179
Town of Big Cypress 72, 83, 85, 87, 91, 92, 105
Troyer 114, 119-124, 126, 128

U

USFWS (U.S. Fish and Wildlife Service) 74, 129, 132-133, 137, 141-142, 184-185

W

Wilson, Jessica 108
Worley, Kathy 40, 42-46, 152, 156, 162

Z

Zadrozny, Tonya 172, 175, 178-179

ACKNOWLEDGEMENTS

I would like to first thank my publisher, Jeff Schlesinger, for his almost constant attention to the drafting and editing of this book. It was written with a hard deadline and his support was unwavering and essential.

I would also like to thank my formatter, Linda Duider, and her amazing ability to coordinate the text and maps into appealing pages. Running into a time problem with professional indexers, she stepped in and took that over earning my undying appreciation.

Greg Willette, at the Conservancy, was helpful in selecting the photographs that appear on the cover of both the hard and soft copies. In that regard, I appreciate the willingness of Dennis Goodman to provide those beautiful images.

Finally, to Rob Moher and all the staff at the Conservancy who willingly gave their time and submitted to interviews and produced clarifying memos to make sure what appears in this book is as factually accurate as it can possibly be, thank you, thank you.

Printed in the USA
CPSIA information can be obtained
at www.ICGtesting.com
JSHW011715300124
56031JS00011B/41/J